A Year in Haiku: Themes and Reflections

Exploring Life, Nature and the Human Spirit

366 Haikus in English with Latin Translations

Harri Hykkö

A Year in Haiku: Themes and Reflections

Exploring Life, Nature and the Human Spirit

366 Haikus in English with Latin Translations

© 2024 Harri Hykkö

Design of cover: Harri Hykkö / BoD
Page layout: Harri Hykkö

Publisher: BoD · Books on Demand GmbH, Helsinki, Finland
Publisher: Libri Plureos GmbH, Hamburg, Germany

ISBN: 978-952-80-8371-9

A Year in Haiku: Themes and Reflections

Exploring Life, Nature and the Human Spirit

How to Read This Book

Welcome to your journey through A Year in Haiku: Daily Reflections. This collection is designed to be read daily, starting from any date you begin. Each day brings a new haiku, offering reflections on various aspects of life, nature, and human experience.

This collection is designed to be enjoyed daily, with each haiku offering a moment of reflection and tranquility. Here are a few tips to help you get the most out of this book:

Start from Today's Date: Rather than beginning at the first haiku, find the haiku that corresponds to today's date and start there. This way, you can immerse yourself in the present moment and follow the cycle naturally.

Daily Reflection: Take a few moments each day to read the haiku and its Latin translation. Reflect on the imagery and emotions it evokes. Allow it to bring a sense of calm and mindfulness to your day.

Read Aloud: Reading the haikus aloud can enhance your connection to the words and their meanings. Try reading both the English and Latin versions to appreciate the rhythm and beauty of each language.

Revisit and Reflect: As you progress through the year, feel free to revisit previous haikus. Reflect on how your understanding and emotions may have evolved over time.

Keep a Journal: Consider keeping a journal of your reflections and thoughts inspired by the daily haikus. This can deepen your engagement and provide a personal record of your journey through the year.

Note on Content:

This collection includes a diverse range of themes and tones:

- **Provocative and Critical Haikus:** Some haikus challenge traditional ideas and critique modern consumption habits. These are meant to provoke thought and encourage deeper reflection on societal norms.

- **Intimate and Personal Haikus:** Other haikus explore intimate, erotic, personal experiences and emotions. They are designed to resonate on a personal level and may evoke strong feelings.

I hope this collection enriches your year with daily moments of contemplation and inspiration.

Remember, this book is a companion to your daily life. Allow it to bring moments of peace, introspection, and connection to the natural world and the timeless wisdom of poetry.

Happy reading!

January 1st

Quiet reflection

Haiku in English:
Quiet mind, still heart,
Whispers of peace in hush,
Spirit finds its way.

Latin Translation:
Mens quieta, cor immotum,
Susurri pacis in silentio,
Spiritus viam invenit.

Reflection Prompt:

How often do you take time for quiet reflection in your daily life? What can you do to create more moments of stillness?

Supplementary Content:

The phrase "Mens quieta, cor immotum" captures the essence of a serene mind and heart. The challenge in translation was to preserve the tranquility conveyed by "quiet mind" and "still heart."

January 2nd

Quiet reflection

Haiku in English:
In stillness, we breathe,
Deep within, the soul awakens,
Tranquil as the dawn.

Latin Translation:
In quiete respiramus,
Intus, anima evigilat,
Tranquilla ut aurora.

Reflection Prompt:

Consider the last time you felt truly tranquil. What practices help you reach a state of inner peace?

Supplementary Content:

"Tranquilla ut aurora" emphasizes the comparison to the dawn, reflecting the calm awakening of the soul. Maintaining this metaphor in translation was crucial to preserve the haiku's imagery.

January 3rd

Quiet reflection
Haiku in English:
Hands together clasped,
Silent words rise to the skies,
Hope in every breath.

Latin Translation:
Manus iunctae,
Verba tacita ad caelos surgunt,
Spes in omni spiritu.

Reflection Prompt:

How does the act of prayer or meditation bring hope into your life?
Reflect on the power of silent communication with the divine.

Supplementary Content:

"Manus iunctae" directly translates to "hands clasped," a simple yet
powerful image of unity in prayer. Ensuring the rise of "silent words"
to the skies retained the haiku's hopeful tone.

January 4th

Quiet reflection
Haiku in English:
Under moon's soft glow,
Meditation's gentle flow,
Peace in every thought.

Latin Translation:
Sub lumine lunae,
Meditationis lenis fluvius,
Pax in omni cogitatione.

Reflection Prompt:

Think about the role of nature in your moments of peace. How does the moon's presence affect your meditation?

Supplementary Content:

"Sub lumine lunae" evokes the soft glow of the moon, a crucial element in setting the tranquil scene. Capturing the "gentle flow" of meditation was important to maintain the haiku's soothing effect.

January 5th

Quiet reflection

Haiku in English:
Candle's flame flickers,
Prayer dances in the shadows,
Faith lights the dark night.

Latin Translation:
Flamma candelae micat,
Oratio in umbris saltat,
Fides noctem obscuram illuminat.

Reflection Prompt:

Consider the symbolism of light in your spiritual practices. How does faith guide you through dark times?

Supplementary Content:

"Flamma candelae micat" conveys the flickering candle flame, a metaphor for the fragile yet persistent nature of faith. Translating the dancing shadows retained the haiku's dynamic imagery.

January 6th

Quiet reflection

Haiku in English:
Morning sun's first light,
Silent prayer, day's new beginning,
Heart opens to grace.

Latin Translation:
Lux prima solis,
Oratio tacita, initium novi diei,
Cor gratiae aperitur.

Reflection Prompt:

How do you start your day with a sense of grace and gratitude? Reflect on the significance of morning rituals.

Supplementary Content:

"Lux prima solis" captures the essence of dawn, while "initium novi diei" emphasizes the fresh start of a new day. The challenge was to preserve the hopeful and gracious tone of the original.

January 7th

Quiet reflection
Haiku in English:
Breath of life flows deep,
Meditation's calm embrace,
Soul's serene refuge.

Latin Translation:
Spiritus vitae profundus fluit,
Complexus quietus meditationis,
Refugium animae serenum.

Reflection Prompt:

Reflect on how meditation serves as a refuge for your soul. What aspects of your practice bring you the most serenity?

Supplementary Content:

"Spiritus vitae profundus fluit" translates to the deep flow of life's breath, emphasizing the meditative calm. Ensuring the "soul's serene refuge" was preserved was key to maintaining the haiku's comforting message.

January 8th

Quiet reflection

Haiku in English:
Whispered prayer at dusk,
Stars emerge, the sky listens,
Eternal stillness.

Latin Translation:
Oratio susurrata crepusculo,
Stellae emergunt, caelum audit,
Aeternum silentium.

Reflection Prompt:

Consider the connection between your prayers and the natural world. How does the night sky influence your spiritual reflections?

Supplementary Content:

"Oratio susurrata crepusculo" conveys the gentle act of whispering prayers at dusk, while "aeternum silentium" captures the profound stillness of the night.

January 9th

Quiet reflection
Haiku in English:
Nature's quiet hymn,
Meditation's gentle touch,
Unity with all.

Latin Translation:
Hymnus quietus naturae,
Tactus lenis meditationis,
Unitas cum omnibus.

Reflection Prompt:

Think about how meditation connects you to nature. In what ways do you experience unity with the world around you?

Supplementary Content:

"Hymnus quietus naturae" translates to nature's quiet hymn, a crucial element in conveying the haiku's theme of harmony with the natural world.

January 10th

Quiet reflection

Haiku in English:
Prayer beneath the trees,
Leaves rustle in soft reply,
Harmony with life.

Latin Translation:
Oratio sub arboribus,
Folia leniter respondent,
Harmonia cum vita.

Reflection Prompt:

Reflect on the role of nature in your spiritual practice. How do the sounds and sights of nature enhance your prayers?

Supplementary Content:

"Oratio sub arboribus" translates to prayer beneath the trees, emphasizing the intimate connection with nature. The challenge was to capture the gentle response of rustling leaves.

January 11th

Quiet reflection

Haiku in English:
Silent night, soft prayer,
Heart whispers to the Divine,
Peaceful dreams unfold.

Latin Translation:
Nox silens, oratio mollis,
Cor Divino susurrat,
Somnia pacifica explicantur.

Reflection Prompt:

Consider how prayer influences your dreams and nighttime reflections. How does it bring peace to your rest?

Supplementary Content:

"Nox silens, oratio mollis" conveys the serene atmosphere of a silent night, while "somnia pacifica explicantur" captures the unfolding of peaceful dreams.

January 12th

Quiet reflection

Haiku in English:
Meditative breath,
Calm waves upon the still lake,
Inner peace restored.

Latin Translation:
Spiritus meditative,
Fluctus placidi super lacum immotum,
Pax interior restituitur.

Reflection Prompt:

Think about the imagery of calm waves in your meditation. How does this visual aid in restoring your inner peace?

Supplementary Content:

"Fluctus placidi super lacum immotum" translates to calm waves upon a still lake, emphasizing the serene imagery that aids in meditation.

January 13th

Quiet reflection

Haiku in English:
Soft rain's gentle fall,
Meditation's rhythmic beat,
Soul cleansed, renewed.

Latin Translation:
Cadentis pluviae lenis,
Ritmicus pulsus meditationis,
Anima purificata, renovata.

Reflection Prompt:

Consider how the sound of rain influences your meditation. How does it contribute to a sense of renewal?

Supplementary Content:

"Cadentis pluviae lenis" captures the gentle fall of rain, while "ritmicus pulsus meditationis" translates to the rhythmic beat of meditation, essential to convey the haiku's theme of renewal.

January 14th

Quiet reflection

Haiku in English:
Prayer's quiet whisper,
In the stillness, answers come,
Faithful heart is healed.

Latin Translation:
Susurrus quietus orationis,
In silentio, responsa veniunt,
Cor fidele sanatur.

Reflection Prompt:

Reflect on how quiet prayer brings answers to your life. In what ways does it heal your heart?

Supplementary Content:

"Susurrus quietus orationis" translates to the quiet whisper of prayer, highlighting the intimate and healing nature of the haiku's message.

January 15th

Quiet reflection

Haiku in English:
Meditation's peace,
Mind and soul in purest light,
Harmony within.

Latin Translation:
Pax meditationis,
Mens et anima in luce pura,
Harmonia intus.

Reflection Prompt:

Think about the inner harmony achieved through meditation. How do mind and soul align in your practice?

Supplementary Content:

"Pax meditationis" translates to meditation's peace, emphasizing the pure light that brings harmony within. Capturing the alignment of mind and soul was crucial to the haiku's overall message.

January 16th

A Sense of Gratitude

Haiku in English:
In morning's first light,
Whispers of thanks fill the air,
Life's gifts everywhere.

Latin Translation:
In prima luce,
Gratias sibilans aerem,
Vitae dona ubique.

Reflection Prompt:

How does the morning light inspire a sense of gratitude in you?
What are the gifts in your life that you often overlook?

Supplementary Content:

"In prima luce" translates to "in the first light," capturing the
freshness and potential of a new day. The process of translating
this haiku involved conveying the serene and reflective quality of
morning and the pervasive presence of life's gifts.

January 17th

A Sense of Gratitude

Haiku in English:
Gentle autumn breeze,
Leaves fall with whispered praises,
Grateful hearts rejoice.

Latin Translation:
Aestas aura mollis,
Folia cadunt laudibus,
Gratiae corda gaudent.

Reflection Prompt:

What does the autumn season represent for you? How do you
express your gratitude during times of change?

Supplementary Content:

"Aestas aura mollis" means "gentle autumn breeze." This
translation emphasizes the tranquility and reflective nature of
autumn, where even the falling leaves can symbolize whispered
praises and the joy of grateful hearts.

January 18th

A Sense of Gratitude

Haiku in English:
Silent night sky, bright,
Stars blink in grateful patterns,
Eternal thanks shine.

Latin Translation:
Noctis caelum tacitum,
Stellae gratiae fulgent,
Aeternae gratiae splendent.

Reflection Prompt:

How do you find comfort and gratitude in the night sky? What do the stars symbolize for you in terms of eternal thanks?

Supplementary Content:

"Noctis caelum tacitum" translates to "silent night sky." The translation aims to capture the serene beauty of a starry night and the enduring gratitude symbolized by the twinkling stars, highlighting the eternal nature of thankfulness.

January 19th

A Sense of Gratitude

Haiku in English:
Hands clasped in thanks,
Warmth of a kindred spirit,
Life's grace in small acts.

Latin Translation:
Manus junctae grates,
Calor animi fraterni,
Vitae gratia actibus.

Reflection Prompt:

Reflect on a recent small act of kindness you experienced. How did it make you feel? How do these small acts contribute to your sense of life's grace?

Supplementary Content:

"Manus junctae grates" translates to "hands clasped in thanks." This haiku and its translation focus on the warmth and connection found in shared gratitude and small acts of kindness, emphasizing life's grace in these moments.

January 20th

A Sense of Gratitude

Haiku in English:
Morning dew glistens,
Nature's quiet gratitude,
Earth's soft embrace.

Latin Translation:
Ros mane splendens,
Gratia tacita naturae,
Terrae mollis amplectitur.

Reflection Prompt:

How does nature express gratitude in subtle ways? Consider the beauty of morning dew—how does it remind you to appreciate the quiet moments in life?

Supplementary Content:

"Ros mane splendens" means "morning dew glistens." This translation captures the delicate beauty of morning dew as a symbol of nature's quiet gratitude. It emphasizes the importance of noticing and appreciating the subtle and gentle expressions of gratitude in the natural world.

January 21st

A Sense of Gratitude

Haiku in English:
Morning light greets me,
Grateful for another day,
Life's gift shines anew.

Latin Translation:
Lux matutina salutat,
Gratus pro alio die,
Donum vitae renidet.

Reflection Prompt:

What are you grateful for when you wake up each morning? How can acknowledging this gratitude set a positive tone for your day?

Supplementary Content:

"Lux matutina salutat" captures the serene and hopeful greeting of morning light. Translating the idea of gratitude for a new day emphasizes the universal appreciation of life's daily renewal.

January 22nd

A Sense of Gratitude

Haiku in English:
Whisper of the wind,
Nature's song fills me with peace,
Gratitude abounds.

Latin Translation:
Susurrus venti,
Carmen naturae me implet pace,
Gratitudo abundat.

Reflection Prompt:

How does nature contribute to your sense of peace and well-being?
Reflect on a moment when the natural world brought you calm.

Supplementary Content:

"Susurrus venti" refers to the gentle whisper of the wind, which is often associated with a sense of peace. Translating this haiku involved capturing the tranquility and gratitude inspired by nature's sounds.

January 23rd

A Sense of Gratitude

Haiku in English:
Warm hands hold my own,
Thankful for the love we share,
Hearts in harmony.

Latin Translation:
Manus calidae me tenent,
Gratus pro amore nostro,
Corda in harmonia.

Reflection Prompt:

Think about someone whose love and support you are thankful for.
How do their actions and presence harmonize with your life?

Supplementary Content:

"Manus calidae" signifies the warmth and comfort of a loving touch.
The translation aims to reflect the deep gratitude felt for shared love
and harmony in relationships.

January 24th

A Sense of Gratitude
Haiku in English:
A friend's kind embrace,
Lifts my spirit, makes me whole,
Gratitude flows deep.

Latin Translation:
Amici benignus amplexus,
Animam levat, me complet,
Gratitudo profunditur.

Reflection Prompt:

Reflect on a moment when a friend's kindness had a significant impact on you. How did it make you feel whole?

Supplementary Content:

"Amici benignus amplexus" translates to a friend's kind embrace. This haiku and its translation focus on the profound sense of gratitude for friendship and its ability to uplift and complete us.

January 25th

A Sense of Gratitude

Haiku in English:
Golden sunset's glow,
Reminds me of life's beauty,
Thankful for each breath.

Latin Translation:
Aurata vesperis lux,
Pulchritudinem vitae monet,
Gratus pro omni spiritu.

Reflection Prompt:

How do moments of natural beauty, like a sunset, remind you to appreciate life? What are you thankful for at the end of each day?

Supplementary Content:

"Aurata vesperis lux" captures the golden light of a sunset, a symbol of life's fleeting beauty. The translation emphasizes the importance of being thankful for every breath and moment.

January 26th

A Sense of Gratitude

Haiku in English:
Rain nourishes earth,
Grateful for the life it brings,
Nature's gentle touch.

Latin Translation:
Pluvia terram nutrit,
Gratus pro vita quam affert,
Tactus lenis naturae.

Reflection Prompt:

Consider the life-giving properties of rain. How does it symbolize renewal and gratitude in your own life?

Supplementary Content:

"Pluvia terram nutrit" translates to rain nourishing the earth. This haiku highlights the gratitude for nature's gentle and sustaining touch, emphasizing the cyclical gift of life.

January 27th

A Sense of Gratitude

Haiku in English:
Songs of morning birds,
Fill my heart with pure delight,
Thankful for their tune.

Latin Translation:
Carmina avium matutinarum,
Corde meo gaudium replent,
Gratus pro eorum cantu.

Reflection Prompt:

How do the sounds of nature, such as birdsong, contribute to your sense of gratitude and joy? Reflect on a morning when you felt uplifted by these sounds.

Supplementary Content:

"Carmina avium matutinarum" refers to the songs of morning birds, which are often a source of delight and tranquility. Translating this haiku involved conveying the joy and gratitude these natural melodies inspire.

January 28th

A Sense of Gratitude

Haiku in English:
Shared laughter with friends,
Moments of joy and kindness,
Gratitude's embrace.

Latin Translation:
Risus cum amicis,
Momentis gaudii et benignitatis,
Gratitudo amplectitur.

Reflection Prompt:

Think about a recent moment of joy shared with friends. How do these experiences contribute to your sense of gratitude?

Supplementary Content:

"Risus cum amicis" captures the essence of shared laughter with friends. This haiku highlights the importance of joy and kindness in friendships and the deep gratitude these moments foster.

January 29th

A Sense of Gratitude

Haiku in English:
Stars in the night sky,
Guide my dreams and calm my fears,
Thankful for their light.

Latin Translation:
Stellae in caelo nocturno,
Somnia mea ducunt et timores sedant,
Gratus pro eorum lumine.

Reflection Prompt:

Reflect on how the night sky and its stars bring you comfort. What dreams and hopes do they inspire in you?

Supplementary Content:

"Stellae in caelo nocturno" translates to stars in the night sky. This haiku conveys the calming and inspiring presence of stars, and the gratitude they evoke for their guiding light.

January 30th

A Sense of Gratitude

Haiku in English:
Soft whispers of trees,
Speak of life's enduring grace,
Grateful for their shade.

Latin Translation:
Susurri arborum mollia,
De gratia vitae loquuntur,
Gratus pro umbra eorum.

Reflection Prompt:

Consider the presence and symbolism of trees in your life. How do they remind you of life's grace and offer you a sense of gratitude?

Supplementary Content:

"Susurri arborum mollia" means the soft whispers of trees. This haiku emphasizes the grace and shelter trees provide, and the gratitude felt for their enduring presence.

January 31st

A Sense of Gratitude
Haiku in English:
Gentle river's flow,
Carries peace to my spirit,
Grateful for its song.

Latin Translation:
Flumen lenis fluxus,
Pacem animae meae fert,
Gratus pro cantu eius.

Reflection Prompt:

How do the sounds of flowing water bring peace to your spirit? Reflect on a moment when a river or stream calmed and inspired you.

Supplementary Content:

"Flumen lenis fluxus" translates to the gentle flow of a river. This haiku captures the soothing effect of a river's song and the gratitude for the peace it brings to the soul.

February 1st

A Sense of Gratitude

Haiku in English:
Hands that heal and care,
Offer hope and bring comfort,
Thankful for their touch.

Latin Translation:
Manus quae sanant et curant,
Spem praebent et solacium afferunt,
Gratus pro tactu eorum.

Reflection Prompt:

Reflect on the people in your life who provide care and comfort. How does their touch bring you hope and solace?

Supplementary Content:

"Manus quae sanant et curant" refers to hands that heal and care. This haiku acknowledges the gratitude for those who offer comfort and hope through their compassionate touch.

February 2nd

A Sense of Gratitude

Haiku in English:
Sunrise paints the sky,
With hues of hope and promise,
Gratitude arises.

Latin Translation:
Aurora caelum pingit,
Spes et promissionis coloribus,
Gratitudo oritur.

Reflection Prompt:

Think about the symbolism of a sunrise. How do its colors of hope and promise inspire gratitude in you each morning?

Supplementary Content:

"Aurora caelum pingit" captures the image of sunrise painting the sky. The translation reflects the rising sense of gratitude inspired by the promise and hope each new day brings.

February 3rd

A Sense of Gratitude

Haiku in English:

Warm fire on cold nights,
Brings us close, kindles our hearts,
Thankful for its glow.

Latin Translation:

Calor ignis in noctibus frigidis,
Nos proximos facit, corda nostra accendit,
Gratus pro splendore eius.

Reflection Prompt:

Consider the comfort of a warm fire on a cold night. How does it bring people together and kindle feelings of gratitude?

Supplementary Content:

"Calor ignis in noctibus frigidis" translates to the warmth of a fire on cold nights. This haiku emphasizes the comfort and closeness a fire provides, and the gratitude for its glow and warmth.

February 4th

A Sense of Gratitude

Haiku in English:
Each moment a gift,
Cherished in the heart's deep well,
Gratitude springs forth.

Latin Translation:
Quodque momentum donum,
In profundo cordis fonte carum,
Gratitudo exsurgit.

Reflection Prompt:

Reflect on the idea that each moment is a gift. How can cherishing these moments in your heart enhance your sense of gratitude?

Supplementary Content:

"Quodque momentum donum" means each moment is a gift. This haiku encourages recognizing the value of every moment and letting gratitude spring forth from the heart's deep well.

February 5th

Old Age

Haiku in English:
Silver strands whisper,
Wisdom earned through many years,
Honor their journey.

Latin Translation:
Argenteae voces,
Sapientia annis parta,
Iter honorant.

Reflection Prompt:

Reflect on a moment when you received advice from an elder. How did their experience shape your understanding of the situation?

Supplementary Content:

In translating "silver strands whisper," the phrase "argenteae voces" captures the poetic imagery of hair and wisdom, emphasizing the respect due to elders' lifelong journeys and accumulated knowledge.

February 6th

Old Age

Haiku in English:
Lines etched by laughter,
Eyes that have seen countless dawns,
Respect their stories.

Latin Translation:
Rugae risus factae,
Oculi auroras spectant,
Eorum fabulas honora.

Reflection Prompt:

Consider the stories shared by your elders. How do their experiences provide a different perspective on the world?

Supplementary Content:

The translation "rugae risus factae" means "lines etched by laughter," highlighting how life's joys and challenges leave a mark. This haiku and its translation focus on the respect for the stories carried by those who have lived through many dawns.

February 7th

Old Age

Haiku in English:
Ancient hands weave tales,
Life's tapestry rich and full,
Revere their legacy.

Latin Translation:
Manus antiqui narrant,
Vitae textus dives plenus,
Eorum legatum venerare.

Reflection Prompt:

Think about the legacy your elders leave behind. How do you preserve and honor their stories and lessons?

Supplementary Content:

"Manus antiqui narrant" translates to "ancient hands weave tales," emphasizing the richness of life's tapestry woven by elders. This translation underscores the importance of venerating their legacy and the depth of their life stories.

February 8th

Old Age

Haiku in English:
Autumn leaves falling,
Graceful in their final dance,
Cherish the elders.

Latin Translation:
Folia autumnalia cadunt,
Gratiose in ultima saltatione,
Senioribus benevole.

Reflection Prompt:

Consider the metaphor of autumn leaves for the elder phase of life. How can you show appreciation for the elders in your life?

Supplementary Content:

"Folia autumnalia cadunt" means "autumn leaves falling," symbolizing the graceful aging process. The translation process highlights the poetic elegance of the final stages of life, encouraging a deep cherishing of elders.

February 9th

Old Age

Haiku in English:
Aged eyes twinkle bright,
Knowledge like a deep river,
Respect flows freely.

Latin Translation:
Oculi aetate micant,
Scientia sicut fluvius altus,
Honor libere fluit.

Reflection Prompt:

Reflect on the depth of knowledge held by the elders you know. How can you tap into this resource and show your respect?

Supplementary Content:

"Oculi aetate micant" translates to "aged eyes twinkle bright," emphasizing the enduring brightness and depth of knowledge in elders. This haiku and its translation focus on the natural flow of respect that should come from recognizing this profound wisdom.

February 10th

Old Age

Haiku in English:
Years etched in their eyes,
Wisdom flows from ancient lips,
Honor elders' words.

Latin Translation:
Anni in oculis sculpti,
Sapientia ex labris antiquis fluit,
Honora verba seniorum.

Reflection Prompt:

What is a piece of advice or wisdom you've received from an elder that has stayed with you? How do you honor and incorporate this wisdom into your daily life?

Supplementary Content:

The translation "anni in oculis sculpti" means "years etched in their eyes," symbolizing the depth of experience elders carry. Translating the reverence for elder wisdom required careful word choices to convey the respect and significance of their life experiences.

February 11th

Old Age

Haiku in English:
In wrinkled hands, tales,
Histories of lives well-lived,
Respect their journey.

Latin Translation:
In manibus rugosis, fabulae,
Historiae vitae bene actae,
Iter eorum respice.

Reflection Prompt:

Consider the stories and experiences that are held in the hands of your elders. What stories from your own family history have shaped who you are today?

Supplementary Content:

"In manibus rugosis" translates to "in wrinkled hands," emphasizing the tactile nature of history and the tangible connection to the past. This haiku and its translation highlight the respect for the journeys and stories that elders carry with them.

February 12th

Old Age

Haiku in English:
Aged voices sing truths,
Lessons learned through time and strife,
Cherish their wisdom.

Latin Translation:
Vocibus aetatis veritates canunt,
Lectiones per tempus et certamen didicimus,
Sapientiam eorum colere.

Reflection Prompt:

Think about a lesson you've learned from an elder. How did their experience and perspective help you understand the world better?

Supplementary Content:

"Vocibus aetatis veritates canunt" means "aged voices sing truths." The translation process for this haiku aimed to encapsulate the melodic and enduring quality of wisdom shared by elders, emphasizing the importance of cherishing their insights.

February 13th

Old Age
Haiku in English:
Old age, a treasure,
Guiding youth with ancient light,
Wisdom's quiet grace.

Latin Translation:
Senectus, thesaurus,
Iuventutem luce antiqua ducens,
Gratia tacita sapientiae.

Reflection Prompt:

Reflect on a moment when you received guidance from an elder. How did their quiet grace and wisdom impact your decision-making?

Supplementary Content:

"Senectus, thesaurus" translates to "old age, a treasure." This haiku and its translation focus on the invaluable guidance elders provide to the youth, comparing their wisdom to a gentle light that illuminates the path forward.

February 14th

Old Age

Haiku in English:
Elders' tales unfold,
Bridges to a distant past,
Honor their wisdom.

Latin Translation:
Fabulae seniorum evolvuntur,
Pontes ad praeteritum remotum,
Sapientiam eorum honora.

Reflection Prompt:

What stories from the past have you learned from your elders? How do these stories help you understand your own place in history?

Supplementary Content:

"Fabulae seniorum evolvuntur" means "elders' tales unfold." Translating this haiku involved capturing the narrative quality of elder wisdom, portraying it as bridges connecting us to the past and emphasizing the importance of honoring these stories.

February 15th

Old Age

Haiku in English:
Silver threads of life,
Weave wisdom in each moment,
Respect their counsel.

Latin Translation:
Argenteae vitae fila,
Sapientiam in unoquoque momento texunt,
Consilium eorum respice.

Reflection Prompt:

Consider the idea of life's experiences as threads woven into a tapestry. How do the silver threads of wisdom from elders contribute to the richness of this tapestry?

Supplementary Content:

"Argenteae vitae fila" translates to "silver threads of life." This haiku and its translation highlight the continuous and intricate nature of wisdom shared by elders, encouraging respect for their counsel as an integral part of life's fabric.

February 16th

Old Age

Haiku in English:
Age brings clarity,
Perspective on life's journey,
Elders' words are gold.

Latin Translation:
Aetas claritatem affert,
Perspectiva in itinere vitae,
Verba seniorum aurum sunt.

Reflection Prompt:

How has the perspective of an elder helped clarify a situation or decision for you? What makes their words so valuable?

Supplementary Content:

"Aetas claritatem affert" means "age brings clarity." This translation aims to convey the sharp insight and invaluable perspective that come with age, portraying elders' words as golden treasures.

February 17th

Old Age

Haiku in English:
Ancient eyes see far,
Through the fog of many years,
Heed their guiding light.

Latin Translation:
Antiqui oculi longe vident,
Per nebulam multorum annorum,
Lucem eorum ducentem audi.

Reflection Prompt:

Think about a time when the guidance of an elder helped you navigate a difficult period. How did their long-term perspective make a difference?

Supplementary Content:

"Antiqui oculi longe vident" translates to "ancient eyes see far." This haiku and its translation emphasize the far-reaching vision of elders, who can see through the complexities of life and offer a guiding light.

February 18th

Old Age

Haiku in English:
Respect the elders,
Guardians of our past dreams,
Teachers of the wise.

Latin Translation:
Seniores respice,
Custodes somniorum nostrorum
praeteritorum,
Magistri sapientium.

Reflection Prompt:

In what ways do you show respect to the elders in your life? How do their past dreams and teachings influence your present and future?

Supplementary Content:

"Seniores respice" means "respect the elders." The translation captures the reverence due to elders, portraying them as guardians of past dreams and teachers who impart wisdom to the wise.

February 19th

Old Age

Haiku in English:
Old age whispers truths,
In their silence, deep lessons,
Honor their long years.

Latin Translation:
Senectus veritates susurrat,
In silentio eorum lectiones profundas,
Honora longos annos eorum.

Reflection Prompt:

Reflect on a quiet moment shared with an elder. What truths or lessons did you glean from their presence or silence?

Supplementary Content:

"Senectus veritates susurrat" translates to "old age whispers truths." This haiku and its translation emphasize the profound lessons that can be learned from the quiet, reflective moments shared with elders, urging us to honor their long years of experience.

February 20th

Love

Haiku in English:
Life's path twists and turns,
Friendship lights the darkest roads,
Hands clasped, hearts entwined.

Latin Translation:
Via vitae vertit,
Amicitia obscura viam illustrat,
Manus junctae, corda ligata.

Reflection Prompt:

Think about a time when a friend helped you through a difficult period. How did their support change your experience?

Supplementary Content:

In translating "Friendship lights the darkest roads," the phrase "Amicitia obscura viam illustrat" was chosen to convey how friendship can illuminate even the most challenging paths in life. This translation aims to preserve the imagery of friendship as a guiding light.

February 21st

Love

Haiku in English:
In life's fleeting hours,
Friendship's warmth defies the cold,
Timeless bonds are forged.

Latin Translation:
In horis vitae,
Calor amicitiae frigus vincit,
Vincula aeterna formantur.

Reflection Prompt:

Reflect on the enduring nature of your closest friendships. How do these relationships provide warmth and comfort in your life?

Supplementary Content:

"Calor amicitiae frigus vincit" translates to "Friendship's warmth defies the cold," highlighting the comforting and enduring nature of true friendships. This translation emphasizes the resilience and timelessness of bonds formed through shared experiences.

February 22nd

Love

Haiku in English:
Beneath the full moon,
Friends share whispers of the heart,
Life's joys gently bloom.

Latin Translation:
Sub luna plena,
Amici cordis sussurant,
Gaudia vitae florent.

Reflection Prompt:

Recall a serene moment shared with friends under the night sky. How did this experience deepen your connection with them?

Supplementary Content:

"Sub luna plena" translates to "Beneath the full moon," capturing the serene and intimate setting where friends share their deepest thoughts. This translation focuses on the quiet and gentle blossoming of life's joys through friendship.

February 23rd

Love

Haiku in English:
Through storms and bright days,
Friendship is the steady sail,
Guiding life's journey.

Latin Translation:
Per tempestates et splendidas dies,
Amicitia velum firmum,
Iter vitae ducit.

Reflection Prompt:

Consider how your friendships have served as a steadying force during both turbulent and peaceful times. In what ways have your friends guided you?

Supplementary Content:

"Amicitia velum firmum" translates to "Friendship is the steady sail," depicting friendship as a reliable and guiding force throughout life's journey. This translation aims to preserve the metaphor of friendship as a steady sail guiding through life's storms and calm seas.

February 24th

Love

Haiku in English:
In laughter and tears,
Life and friendship interlace,
Moments shared, treasured.

Latin Translation:
In risu et lacrimis,
Vita et amicitia texuntur,
Momenta communia, pretiosa.

Reflection Prompt:

Think about the shared moments of joy and sorrow with your friends. How do these experiences intertwine your lives and make them richer?

Supplementary Content:

"In risu et lacrimis" means "In laughter and tears," highlighting the intertwined nature of life and friendship through both joyous and sorrowful times. This translation emphasizes the value of shared moments and how they are treasured in the tapestry of life.

February 25th

Stress

Haiku in English:
Haste and tension reign,
In stillness, calm waters flow,
Peace found in forests.

Latin Translation:
Festinatio regnat,
In quiete aquae fluunt,
Pax in silvis invenitur.

Reflection Prompt:

Think about a time when you felt overwhelmed by haste and tension. How might spending time in nature help you find peace and calm?

Supplementary Content:

"In quiete aquae fluunt" (In stillness, calm waters flow) reflects the idea that nature's tranquility can help soothe our hurried minds, a concept beautifully captured in both English and Latin.

February 26th

Stress

Haiku in English:
Stress and smog conspire,
Meditation clears the mind,
Clean air heals the soul.

Latin Translation:
Stressus et fumus coniurant,
Meditatio mentem purgat,
Aeris puri animam sanat.

Reflection Prompt:

Consider how environmental factors like smog affect your mental state. How can practices like meditation help counteract these negative effects?

Supplementary Content:

"Meditatio mentem purgat" (Meditation clears the mind) emphasizes the cleansing power of meditation, especially in environments where physical and mental pollutants are prevalent.

February 27th

Stress

Haiku in English:
Anxiety grips tight,
Forests whisper soothing peace,
Calm through nature's breath.

Latin Translation:
Anxietas arcte tenet,
Silvae pacem susurrant,
Quies per naturae flatum.

Reflection Prompt:

Reflect on a time when anxiety felt overwhelming. How can spending time in a forest or natural setting help alleviate that anxiety?

Supplementary Content:

"Silvae pacem susurrant" (Forests whisper soothing peace) captures the essence of how nature can communicate peace to us, providing a gentle reminder of the calming effects of the natural world.

February 28th

Stress

Haiku in English:
Mental strain and smog,
Clean streams, thoughts clear, heart finds peace,
Nature's cure unfolds.

Latin Translation:
Fatigatio mentis et fumus,
Rivi puri, mens clara, cor pacem invenit,
Naturae cura panditur.

Reflection Prompt:

Think about the mental strain you experience in polluted environments. How do clean natural settings help clear your mind and bring peace to your heart?

Supplementary Content:

"Rivi puri, mens clara, cor pacem invenit" (Clean streams, thoughts clear, heart finds peace) illustrates how nature's purity can positively impact our mental and emotional well-being.

February 29th

Stress

Haiku in English:
Pollution chokes life,
Inaction's grace brings fresh air,
Breathe in the forest.

Latin Translation:
Pollutio vitam suffocat,
Gratia inertia aerem recentem affert,
Spira in silva.

Reflection Prompt:

Consider the impact of pollution on your life. How can taking time to rest and embrace nature provide you with the fresh air and renewal you need?

Supplementary Content:

"Gratia inertia aerem recentem affert" (Inaction's grace brings fresh air) suggests that sometimes, simply pausing and doing nothing in a natural setting can be incredibly rejuvenating.

March 1st

Stress

Haiku in English:
Diseases spread wide,
Calm mind and pure waters heal,
Nature's balm prevails.

Latin Translation:
Morbi late diffusi,
Mens tranquilla et aquae purae sanant,
Naturae balsamum praevalet.

Reflection Prompt:

Reflect on the healing power of nature during times of illness. How do calm environments and clean water contribute to your overall well-being?

Supplementary Content:

"Mens tranquilla et aquae purae sanant" (Calm mind and pure waters heal) highlights the therapeutic effects of natural elements on both physical and mental health.

March 2nd

Stress

Haiku in English:
Tension fills the air,
Fragrant woods and mindful breath,
Ease the troubled soul.

Latin Translation:
Tensio aerem implet,
Silvae fragrantia et respiratio tranquilla,
Animam turbulentam leniunt.

Reflection Prompt:

Think about how tension affects your body and mind. How can the scents and atmosphere of a forest, combined with mindful breathing, help ease your troubled soul?

Supplementary Content:

"Silvae fragrantia et respiratio tranquilla" (Fragrant woods and mindful breath) emphasizes the multi-sensory experience of nature's healing power, from scent to breath.

March 3rd

Stress

Haiku in English:
Stress and filth abound,
Meditative forest walks,
Bring the spirit calm.

Latin Translation:
Stressus et sordes ubique,
Meditativa silvae itinera,
Spiritum tranquillitatem afferunt.

Reflection Prompt:

Reflect on the stress and dirtiness of urban environments. How do meditative walks in the forest help bring calm and tranquility to your spirit?

Supplementary Content:

"Meditativa silvae itinera" (Meditative forest walks) conveys the idea that walking in nature can be a meditative practice, bringing calm and peace to the mind and spirit.

March 4th

Stress

Haiku in English:
Fatigue weighs heavy,
Crystal streams and quiet thoughts,
Revive weary hearts.

Latin Translation:
Fatigatio gravis,
Flumina crystallina et cogitationes quietae,
Corda fessa renovant.

Reflection Prompt:

Think about the times when you feel most fatigued. How can spending time by clear streams and engaging in quiet reflection help revive your weary heart?

Supplementary Content:

"Flumina crystallina et cogitationes quietae" (Crystal streams and quiet thoughts) highlights the restorative power of nature's beauty and stillness on our emotional and mental states.

March 5th

Stress

Haiku in English:
Haste and illness rage,
In the forest's cool embrace,
Find healing and peace.

Latin Translation:
Festinatio et morbus saeviunt,
In amplexu frigido silvae,
Sanitatem et pacem invenire.

Reflection Prompt:

Consider the impact of haste and illness on your life. How can the cool embrace of a forest help you find healing and peace?

Supplementary Content:

"In amplexu frigido silvae" (In the forest's cool embrace) captures the comforting and healing properties of nature, suggesting that even in the face of haste and illness, peace and recovery can be found in natural settings.

March 6th

Stress

Haiku in English:
Endless rush of days,
Calm found in still meditation,
Mind's peace reclaimed slow.

Latin Translation:
Dies in fine currunt,
Quies in meditatione,
Pax mentis lente recipitur.

Reflection Prompt:

Reflect on how often you feel rushed during your day. How might incorporating moments of still meditation help you reclaim your mental peace?

Supplementary Content:

The Latin phrase "Pax mentis lente recipitur" (Mind's peace reclaimed slow) emphasizes the gradual process of finding calm and peace through meditation.

March 7th

Stress

Haiku in English:
Anxiety reigns,
Deep breaths and quiet moments,
Ease the troubled mind.

Latin Translation:
Anxietas regnat,
Profunda respiratio et quies,
Mentes turbatae leniuntur.

Reflection Prompt:

When anxiety takes over, what methods do you use to find relief? How can deep breathing and quiet moments help ease your mind?

Supplementary Content:

"Profunda respiratio et quies" (Deep breaths and quiet moments) highlights the effectiveness of simple yet profound practices in alleviating anxiety.

March 8th

Stress

Haiku in English:
Stress in every breath,
Stillness whispers to the heart,
Find peace in silence.

Latin Translation:
Stressus in omni spiritu,
Silentium cordi susurrat,
Pacem in silentio invenire.

Reflection Prompt:

Think about a recent stressful situation. How can listening to the whispers of stillness help you find peace in such moments?

Supplementary Content:

"Silentium cordi susurrat" (Stillness whispers to the heart) illustrates the subtle yet powerful impact of stillness on our inner peace.

March 9th

Stress

Haiku in English:
Tension grips us tight,
Meditative thoughts bring calm,
Release in stillness.

Latin Translation:
Tensio nos tenet,
Meditationes pacem afferunt,
Quies relaxationem affert.

Reflection Prompt:

Reflect on the ways tension affects your body and mind. How might meditative thoughts and stillness help you release this tension?

Supplementary Content:

"Meditationes pacem afferunt" (Meditative thoughts bring calm) underscores the role of mindful thinking in achieving relaxation and peace.

March 10th

Stress

Haiku in English:
Mental fatigue reigns,
In inefficiency's grace,
Rest renews the soul.

Latin Translation:
Fatigatio mentis regnat,
In inefficacia gratia,
Quies animam renovat.

Reflection Prompt:

When was the last time you felt mentally exhausted? How can embracing inefficiency and allowing yourself to rest renew your soul?

Supplementary Content:

"In inefficacia gratia" (In inefficiency's grace) suggests that allowing yourself to be inefficient can lead to much-needed rest and mental rejuvenation.

March 11th

Stress

Haiku in English:
Haste makes moments blur,
Slow down, breathe in beauty's calm,
Life's essence savored.

Latin Translation:
Festinatio momenta obfuscans,
Lente, pulchritudinem respirans,
Essentia vitae gustata.

Reflection Prompt:

Recall a time when haste made you miss out on the beauty of the moment. How can slowing down help you savor the essence of life?

Supplementary Content:

"Pulchritudinem respirans" (Breathe in beauty's calm) conveys the importance of taking time to appreciate the beauty around us and how it enriches our lives.

March 12th

Stress

Haiku in English:
Thoughts race endlessly,
Mind control brings gentle peace,
Chaos fades to calm.

Latin Translation:
Cogitationes sine fine currunt,
Mens imperium pacem affert,
Chaos in quietem mutat.

Reflection Prompt:

Think about how often your thoughts race uncontrollably. How can mind control techniques bring you gentle peace and transform chaos into calm?

Supplementary Content:

"Mens imperium pacem affert" (Mind control brings gentle peace) highlights the power of mental discipline in achieving a state of calm and tranquility.

March 13th

Stress

Haiku in English:
Stress and strain collide,
Meditation's soft embrace,
Holds the storm at bay.

Latin Translation:
Stressus et labor colliduntur,
Meditationis mollis amplexus,
Tempestatas tenet sinus.

Reflection Prompt:

Reflect on a stressful event where you felt overwhelmed. How can meditation's soft embrace help you hold the storm at bay?

Supplementary Content:

"Meditationis mollis amplexus" (Meditation's soft embrace) suggests the gentle yet firm way in which meditation can help manage stress and strain.

March 14th

Stress

Haiku in English:
Anxiety's grip,
Loosened by mindful stillness,
Serenity blooms.

Latin Translation:
Gravis anxietatis,
A quiete mentis soluta,
Serenitas floret.

Reflection Prompt:

Consider a time when anxiety had a tight grip on you. How can mindful stillness help loosen this grip and allow serenity to bloom?

Supplementary Content:

"A quiete mentis soluta" (Loosened by mindful stillness) emphasizes the freeing effect of stillness on anxiety, allowing serenity to flourish.

March 15th

Stress

Haiku in English:
In haste we find loss,
In inaction, life's pure joy,
Stillness breathes new life.

Latin Translation:
In festinatione damnum invenimus,
In inertia, pura vita gaudium,
Quies novam vitam spirat.

Reflection Prompt:

Think about what you lose when you rush through life. How can embracing inaction and stillness help you find pure joy and breathe new life into your experiences?

Supplementary Content:

"In inertia, pura vita gaudium" (In inaction, life's pure joy) highlights the paradox that sometimes, doing nothing can lead to the most profound joy and revitalization.

March 16th

Stress

Haiku in English:
Haste consumes the day,
Silent breath brings peace anew,
In stillness, we heal.

Latin Translation:
Festinatio diem consumit,
Tacitus spiritus pacem novam affert,
In quiete sanamur.

Reflection Prompt:

Reflect on a moment today when you felt overwhelmed by haste. How can incorporating a minute of silent breathing into your daily routine help restore your peace?

Supplementary Content:

The phrase "Tacitus spiritus pacem novam affert" (Silent breath brings peace anew) underscores the importance of pausing and breathing to reset and rejuvenate amidst a busy day.

March 17th

Stress

Haiku in English:
Tension clouds the mind,
Meditation clears the way,
Thoughts in calm control.

Latin Translation:
Tensio mentem obscurat,
Meditatio viam purgat,
Cogitationes in quiete moderantur.

Reflection Prompt:

When was the last time you felt your thoughts clouded by tension? How might meditation help you find clarity?

Supplementary Content:

"Meditatio viam purgat" translates to "Meditation clears the way," emphasizing how meditation can help clear mental pathways, allowing for calm and controlled thoughts.

March 18th

Stress

Haiku in English:
Anxiety reigns,
Gentle focus calms the storm,
Peace found in stillness.

Latin Translation:
Anxietas regnat,
Mitis focus tempestatem sedat,
Quies in quiete invenitur.

Reflection Prompt:

Consider a time when anxiety felt overwhelming. How can practicing gentle focus bring calm into your life?

Supplementary Content:

"Mitis focus tempestatem sedat" (Gentle focus calms the storm) illustrates how a soft, steady focus can alleviate anxiety and bring about a sense of calm.

March 19th

Stress

Haiku in English:
Mental fatigue fades,
Through mindful breaths and stillness,
Power in repose.

Latin Translation:
Fatigatio mentis evanescit,
Per anhelitus tranquillos et quietem,
Potestas in requie.

Reflection Prompt:

Think about how often you feel mentally fatigued. What mindful practices can you introduce to help fade this fatigue?

Supplementary Content:

The phrase "Per anhelitus tranquillos et quietem" (Through mindful breaths and stillness) emphasizes the rejuvenating power of mindful breathing and rest in overcoming mental fatigue.

March 20th

Stress

Haiku in English:
Constant rush depletes,
Beauty found in slowing down,
Strength in quiet pause.

Latin Translation:
Continuus impetus exhaurit,
Pulchritudo in tarditate reperta,
Robur in quieta pausa.

Reflection Prompt:

Recall the last time you paused to appreciate something beautiful. How can you find more moments to slow down and regain strength?

Supplementary Content:

"Pulchritudo in tarditate reperta" (Beauty found in slowing down) suggests that taking the time to pause and observe can reveal beauty and provide strength in moments of quiet.

March 21st

Stress

Haiku in English:
Stress fills busy days,
Meditation empties it,
Calm in quiet thought.

Latin Translation:
Stress dies occupatos implet,
Meditatio eam exhaurit,
Quies in tranquilla cogitatione.

Reflection Prompt:

Think about the stress you encounter daily. How might regular meditation help to empty this stress and bring calm?

Supplementary Content:

"Meditatio eam exhaurit" (Meditation empties it) highlights how meditation can act as a release valve for stress, promoting calm through quiet reflection.

March 22nd

Stress

Haiku in English:
Haste and rush consume,
In inefficiency's grace,
Peace is rediscovered.

Latin Translation:
Festinatio et impetus consumunt,
In gratia inefficienciae,
Pax reperta est.

Reflection Prompt:

Reflect on a time when taking things slow led to a peaceful outcome. How can you embrace the grace of inefficiency more often?

Supplementary Content:

"In gratia inefficienciae" (In inefficiency's grace) conveys that sometimes allowing yourself to be less efficient can lead to discovering peace and tranquility.

March 23rd

Stress

Haiku in English:
Anxiety grips tight,
Gentle stillness loosens bonds,
Freedom in calm breath.

Latin Translation:
Anxietas tenet fortiter,
Mitis quies vincula resolvit,
Libertas in tranquillo spiritu.

Reflection Prompt:

How has anxiety held you back recently? What role can gentle stillness and calm breathing play in loosening those bonds?

Supplementary Content:

"Mitis quies vincula resolvit" (Gentle stillness loosens bonds) underscores the power of gentle stillness in freeing oneself from the grips of anxiety.

March 24th

Stress

Haiku in English:
Mental strain weighs down,
Inaction lifts the burden,
Strength through restful peace.

Latin Translation:
Onus mentis gravat,
Inertia onus levat,
Robur per pacem quietam.

Reflection Prompt:

Consider how taking a break has helped you in the past. How can you incorporate restful peace into your daily routine to relieve mental strain?

Supplementary Content:

"Inertia onus levat" (Inaction lifts the burden) illustrates how taking time to rest and doing nothing can significantly reduce mental strain and provide strength through peace.

March 25th

Stress

Haiku in English:
Tension's heavy hand,
Falls away with mindful rest,
Calm restores the soul.

Latin Translation:
Gravis manus tensionis,
Cum quiete tranquilla recedit,
Quies animam renovat.

Reflection Prompt:

Think about a time when mindful rest helped alleviate tension. How can you make mindful rest a regular part of your routine?

Supplementary Content:

"Cum quiete tranquilla recedit" (Falls away with mindful rest) highlights how mindful rest can dissipate tension and restore a sense of calm and well-being to the soul.

March 26th

Functional friendship

Haiku in English:
Apartments so small,
Friends are distant, roles defined,
True bonds hard to find.

Latin Translation:
Parvae domus,
Amici remoti, munera,
Veri nexus difficiles.

Reflection Prompt:

Consider your living space and social connections. How do the size of your home and the roles you play affect your ability to form true bonds?

Supplementary Content:

The phrase "Parvae domus" (small homes) emphasizes how limited physical space can contribute to feelings of isolation, making it harder to form deep, meaningful connections.

March 27th

Functional friendship

Haiku in English:
Business ties prevail,
Functional friends fill the void,
Loneliness persists.

Latin Translation:
Nexus negotii,
Amici munerarii,
Solitudinem manet.

Reflection Prompt:

Reflect on the nature of your friendships. Are they primarily based on mutual benefits or true emotional support? How does this impact your sense of loneliness?

Supplementary Content:

"Nexus negotii" (business ties) and "amici munerarii" (functional friends) illustrate how professional relationships can sometimes overshadow genuine friendships, leaving a lingering sense of loneliness.

March 28th

Functional friendship

Haiku in English:
No real friends nearby,
Small homes echo silent cries,
Connections feel thin.

Latin Translation:
Nulli amici propinqui,
Parvae domus clamores tacent,
Nexus tenuis.

Reflection Prompt:

Think about the emotional impact of having no close friends nearby. How do your surroundings amplify or mitigate these feelings?

Supplementary Content:

"Nulli amici propinqui" (no real friends nearby) and "parvae domus clamores tacent" (small homes echo silent cries) together highlight the isolation that can come from both physical and emotional distance.

March 29th

Functional friendship

Haiku in English:
Relatives afar,
Functional friends at the door,
Heart's warmth feels so cold.

Latin Translation:
Propinqui longe,
Amici munerarii,
Calor cordis frigidus.

Reflection Prompt:

Consider how the physical distance from relatives and reliance on functional friends affects your emotional warmth. What can you do to bring more genuine warmth into your life?

Supplementary Content:

"Propinqui longe" (relatives afar) underscores the emotional gap that physical distance from loved ones can create, while "calor cordis frigidus" (heart's warmth feels so cold) poignantly expresses the resulting emotional chill.

March 30th

Functional friendship

Haiku in English:
Professional ties,
Friendship masked by benefit,
True warmth, a lost dream.

Latin Translation:
Nexus professionales,
Amicitia beneficio tecta,
Verus calor somnium perditum.

Reflection Prompt:

Reflect on how professional relationships may mask the need for true emotional connections. How can you navigate these relationships to find or maintain genuine warmth?

Supplementary Content:

"Amicitia beneficio tecta" (friendship masked by benefit) reveals the superficial nature of some professional relationships, hinting at the deeper, more authentic connections we often yearn for.

March 31st

Functional friendship

Haiku in English:
Small homes, big distance,
Friends for roles, not for the heart,
Loneliness deepens.

Latin Translation:
Parvae domus, magna distantia,
Amici pro muneribus, non pro corde,
Solitudinem profunditur.

Reflection Prompt:

Think about how your environment and the roles you play in others' lives influence your feelings of loneliness. How can you bridge the emotional distance?

Supplementary Content:

"Amici pro muneribus, non pro corde" (friends for roles, not for the heart) underscores how functional relationships, rather than heartfelt ones, contribute to deeper loneliness.

April 1st

Functional friendship
Haiku in English:
Functional smiles,
Business lunches, cold handshakes,
Yearning for real touch.

Latin Translation:
Sibilans munerarii,
Prandia negotia, manus frigidae,
Tactus verus desideratus.

Reflection Prompt:

Consider the difference between functional interactions and genuine connections. How does physical touch or the lack thereof affect your emotional state?

Supplementary Content:

"Manus frigidae" (cold handshakes) and "tactus verus desideratus" (yearning for real touch) highlight the emotional void that superficial interactions can leave.

April 2nd

Functional friendship

Haiku in English:
Distance in the heart,
Functional friends can't bridge gaps,
True friendship is lost.

Latin Translation:
Distantia in corde,
Amici munerarii fossas non iungunt,
Vera amicitia perdita.

Reflection Prompt:

Reflect on the gaps in your emotional connections. How can you move beyond functional friendships to build true, meaningful relationships?

Supplementary Content:

"Distantia in corde" (distance in the heart) conveys the emotional chasms that functional friendships cannot bridge, emphasizing the loss of true friendship.

April 3rd

Functional friendship

Haiku in English:
Apartments, lone cells,
Relatives in distant lands,
Fake friends, empty words.

Latin Translation:
Parvae domus, cellulae solitariae,
Propinqui in terris remotis,
Amici falsi, verba vacua.

Reflection Prompt:

Consider the impact of living in small, isolated spaces on your social connections. How do fake friendships and empty words affect your sense of belonging?

Supplementary Content:

"Parvae domus, cellulae solitariae" (small homes, lone cells) and "amici falsi, verba vacua" (fake friends, empty words) depict the isolation and superficiality that can pervade modern living.

April 4th

Functional friendship

Haiku in English:
True friends far away,
Small homes echo with silence,
Business masks the void.

Latin Translation:
Veri amici longe,
Parvae domus silentium resonant,
Negotium vacuum tegit.

Reflection Prompt:

Reflect on how the physical and emotional distance from true friends impacts you. What steps can you take to fill the void with genuine connections?

Supplementary Content:

"Veri amici longe" (true friends far away) and "negotium vacuum tegit" (business masks the void) capture the essence of longing for true connections in a world filled with superficial interactions.

April 5th

Functional friendship
Haiku in English:
Small homes, empty nights,
Business friends fade with sunset,
Loneliness creeps in.

Latin Translation:
Parvae domus, vacuae noctes,
Amici negotii occidente solis evanescunt,
Solitudinem insidet.

Reflection Prompt:

Consider a time when professional relationships have given way to loneliness. How do personal connections differ in their lasting impact?

Supplementary Content:

"Parvae domus" highlights the small, often isolating living spaces. The translation process aimed to maintain the essence of loneliness creeping in as the superficiality of business friendships fades away.

April 6th

Functional friendship
Haiku in English:
Relatives afar,
Functional friends drift away,
Hobbies fill the void.

Latin Translation:
Propinqui longe,
Amici munerarii discedunt,
Hobby vacuum replent.

Reflection Prompt:

Reflect on the role hobbies play in your life. How have they helped you cope with feelings of isolation or disconnection?

Supplementary Content:

"Propinqui longe" signifies distant relatives, underscoring the physical and emotional gaps. This haiku emphasizes how hobbies can fill emotional voids left by distant or functional relationships.

April 7th

Functional friendship

Haiku in English:
Work ends, night is still,
Business ties now shadows cast,
Seek hobbies, find friends.

Latin Translation:
Labor finit, nox tranquilla,
Nexus negotii umbras iaciunt,
Quaere hobbies, invenire amicos.

Reflection Prompt:

Think about the transition from a busy work life to quiet nights. How can hobbies facilitate the formation of deeper, more meaningful friendships?

Supplementary Content:

"Nexus negotii umbras iaciunt" translates to business ties casting shadows, reflecting their transient nature. This haiku encourages seeking hobbies as a way to discover true friendships.

April 8th

Functional friendship

Haiku in English:
Small flats, distant kin,
Benefit-based friendships wane,
Hobbies spark new bonds.

Latin Translation:
Parvae domus, propinqui longi,
Amicitiae beneficio fundatae languescunt,
Hobby novos nexus accendunt.

Reflection Prompt:

Consider the limitations of benefit-based friendships. How have hobbies sparked new, genuine bonds in your life?

Supplementary Content:

"Amicitiae beneficio fundatae" points to friendships based on convenience or benefit. This haiku shows how hobbies can ignite new and more authentic connections.

April 9th

Functional friendship

Haiku in English:
Functional smiles fade,
Apartment walls close in tight,
Hobbies bring solace.

Latin Translation:
Sibilans munerarii evanescunt,
Parietes domorum arctantur,
Hobby solatium afferunt.

Reflection Prompt:

Reflect on a time when superficial interactions left you feeling isolated. How did engaging in hobbies bring comfort or joy?

Supplementary Content:

"Sibilans munerarii" means functional smiles, capturing the superficiality of certain relationships. The haiku and its translation stress how hobbies provide solace against the closing walls of isolation.

April 10th

Functional friendship

Haiku in English:
Work's end, silence falls,
Business ties now memories,
Hobbies find true friends.

Latin Translation:
Labor finis, silentium cadit,
Nexus negotii nunc memoriae,
Hobby veros amicos invenire.

Reflection Prompt:

Think about the end of a busy day. How do hobbies help you transition from professional to personal fulfillment?

Supplementary Content:

"Nexus negotii nunc memoriae" translates to business ties now being memories. This haiku illustrates how hobbies can help find true friends beyond professional circles.

April 11th

Functional friendship

Haiku in English:
Apartments echo,
Friends shift with each new title,
Hobbies hold true bonds.

Latin Translation:
Parvae domus resonant,
Amici cum novis titulis mutantur,
Hobby veros nexus tenent.

Reflection Prompt:

Reflect on how friendships have shifted with job changes or new roles. How have hobbies provided stable and true connections?

Supplementary Content:

"Amici cum novis titulis mutantur" refers to friends changing with new titles. This haiku points out the reliability of hobbies in holding true bonds amid professional shifts.

April 12th

Functional friendship

Haiku in English:
Far kin, fleeting friends,
Profession masks deep longing,
Hobbies, friends emerge.

Latin Translation:
Propinqui longi, amici fugaces,
Professio profundum desiderium tegit,
Hobby, amici emergunt.

Reflection Prompt:

Consider how your profession might mask deeper longings for connection. How have hobbies revealed true friendships?

Supplementary Content:

"Professio profundum desiderium tegit" highlights how professions can hide deep desires for genuine connections. This haiku showcases how hobbies allow those true friendships to emerge.

April 13th

Functional friendship

Haiku in English:
Small homes, lonely nights,
Business friends soon disappear,
Hobbies, lasting ties.

Latin Translation:
Parvae domus, solitariae noctes,
Amici negotii cito evanescunt,
Hobby, diuturni nexus.

Reflection Prompt:

Think about the fleeting nature of business friendships. How have hobbies contributed to creating lasting relationships?

Supplementary Content:

"Amici negotii cito evanescunt" means business friends soon disappear, emphasizing their temporary nature. The haiku underlines how hobbies forge lasting ties.

April 14th

Functional friendship

Haiku in English:

No true friends nearby,
Functional bonds fade with work,
Hobbies light new paths.

Latin Translation:

Nulli veri amici prope,
Nexus munerarii cum labore evanescunt,
Hobby novas vias illuminant.

Reflection Prompt:

Reflect on the absence of true friends nearby. How have hobbies illuminated new paths to meaningful connections?

Supplementary Content:

"Nexus munerarii cum labore evanescunt" translates to functional bonds fading with work. This haiku highlights how hobbies can light new paths to fulfilling friendships.

April 15th

Awareness

Haiku in English:
Advertisements loud,
Consumption grips anxious hearts,
Nature cries unseen.

Latin Translation:
Reclamationes clarae,
Consumptio corda anxia premit,
Natura clamat invisibilis.

Reflection Prompt:

Reflect on how advertisements influence our daily decisions and awareness. How can we become more conscious of their impact on our environment?

Supplementary Content:

The Latin translation "Reclamationes clarae" captures the loudness and omnipresence of advertisements. This haiku highlights the often unseen and unheard cries of nature amidst the noise of consumerism.

April 16th

Awareness

Haiku in English:
Pollution ignored,
Climate change, a distant threat,
Youth demand the truth.

Latin Translation:
Pollutio neglecta,
Mutatio climatis, periculum remotum,
Iuventus veritatem postulant.

Reflection Prompt:

Why is climate change often perceived as a distant threat? How can young voices make a difference in bringing attention to this urgent issue?

Supplementary Content:

"Pollutio neglecta" underscores how pollution is frequently overlooked. This haiku emphasizes the rising awareness and demand for truth among the youth regarding environmental issues.

April 17th

Awareness
Haiku in English:
Anxiety reigns,
Marketing fills every mind,
Brave youth seek the change.

Latin Translation:
Anxietas regnat,
Mercatura mentes omnes implet,
Iuvenes fortes mutationem quaerunt.

Reflection Prompt:

How does constant marketing contribute to societal anxiety? What role do young people play in challenging and changing these narratives?

Supplementary Content:

"Mercatura mentes omnes implet" reflects how marketing saturates our thoughts. This haiku points to the courage and determination of young individuals seeking change against overwhelming odds.

April 18th

Awareness

Haiku in English:
In the grip of ads,
Few see the world's true struggles,
Youth rise with strong hearts.

Latin Translation:
In vinculo adclamationum,
Pauci veras mundi luctas vident,
Iuvenes cordibus fortibus surgunt.

Reflection Prompt:

Consider the ways advertisements distract us from global issues. How can young people raise awareness about these critical matters?

Supplementary Content:

"In vinculo adclamationum" describes being trapped by ads. This haiku highlights the resilience and strength of youth in addressing and rising above the world's true struggles.

April 19th

Awareness

Haiku in English:
Communities form,
Brave young souls unite for change,
Hope grows in their hands.

Latin Translation:
Communitates formantur,
Iuvenes fortes pro mutatione coniungunt,
Spes in manibus crescit.

Reflection Prompt:

Reflect on the power of community in driving change. How do young people inspire hope and action in their communities?

Supplementary Content:

"Communitates formantur" emphasizes the formation of communities. This haiku celebrates the unity and hope that young people bring through collective action.

April 20th

Awareness

Haiku in English:
Nature's plight ignored,
Brave voices rise for justice,
Youth bring light anew.

Latin Translation:
Casus naturae neglectus,
Fortes voces pro iustitia surgunt,
Iuventus lumen novum afferunt.

Reflection Prompt:

Why is it important to listen to the voices calling for environmental justice? How do young activists bring new light to these issues?

Supplementary Content:

"Fortes voces pro iustitia surgunt" highlights the rise of brave voices. This haiku underscores the role of youth in advocating for justice and illuminating neglected environmental issues.

April 21st

Awareness

Haiku in English:
Consumption's tight grip,
Polluted skies fade from thought,
Youth demand clean air.

Latin Translation:
Tenax consumptio,
Caeli pollutio a mente recedunt,
Iuventus aerem purum postulant.

Reflection Prompt:

How does consumerism contribute to environmental degradation? What steps can be taken to prioritize clean air and a healthy environment?

Supplementary Content:

"Caeli pollutio a mente recedunt" reflects the fading concern for polluted skies. This haiku focuses on the urgent demand from youth for clean air and a healthier planet.

April 22nd

Awareness

Haiku in English:
Anxiety rules,
Ads whisper in every ear,
Youth break free with hope.

Latin Translation:
Anxietas regnat,
Adclamationes in omnibus auribus
susurrant,
Iuventus cum spe liberantur.

Reflection Prompt:

Consider how pervasive advertising contributes to collective anxiety. How can young people break free from this cycle and foster hope?

Supplementary Content:

"Adclamationes in omnibus auribus susurrant" describes the constant presence of ads. This haiku highlights the hope and liberation that youth bring by challenging these pervasive influences.

April 23rd

Awareness

Haiku in English:
Lost in constant ads,
Few notice the world's decline,
Youth call for action.

Latin Translation:
In adclamationibus constantibus perditi,
Pauci mundi declinationem animadvertunt,
Iuventus ad agendum vocant.

Reflection Prompt:

Reflect on how constant advertising can distract from environmental decline. What actions can young people take to bring about change?

Supplementary Content:

"In adclamationibus constantibus perditi" emphasizes being lost in a sea of ads. This haiku stresses the call to action from youth to address and mitigate the world's decline.

April 24th

Awareness
Haiku in English:
Pollution persists,
Climate change, a muffled cry,
Youth hear and respond.

Latin Translation:
Pollutio perseverat,
Mutatio climatis, clamorem submissa,
Iuventus audiunt et respondent.

Reflection Prompt:

Why is it crucial to heed the muted cries of climate change? How do young people respond to these urgent calls?

Supplementary Content:

"Clamorem submissa" depicts the muffled cry of climate change. This haiku highlights the responsiveness and activism of youth in addressing ongoing environmental issues.

April 25th

Awareness

Haiku in English:
Brave young hearts unite,
Communities born of hope,
Change begins with them.

Latin Translation:
Cordia iuvenum fortia coniunguntur,
Communitates spe natae,
Mutatio cum eis incipit.

Reflection Prompt:

Consider the significance of unity among young people in driving change. How do communities founded on hope create lasting impact?

Supplementary Content:

"Cordia iuvenum fortia coniunguntur" illustrates the unity of brave young hearts. This haiku celebrates the birth of hopeful communities and the transformative power of youth-led change.

April 26th

Awareness

Haiku in English:
Nature needs voices,
Youth demand a cleaner world,
Action fuels their cause.

Latin Translation:
Natura vocibus indiget,
Iuventus mundum puriorem postulant,
Actio causam eorum alit.

Reflection Prompt:

Reflect on the importance of advocating for nature. How does the proactive stance of youth inspire broader environmental action?

Supplementary Content:

"Natura vocibus indiget" highlights nature's need for advocacy. This haiku emphasizes the crucial role of youth in demanding a cleaner world and fueling their cause with action.

April 27th

Love

Haiku in English:
Hand in hand we walk,
Through life's sorrows and its joys,
Love's enduring bond.

Latin Translation:
Manu in manu ambulamus,
Per vitae luctus et laetitia,
Vinculum amoris durat.

Reflection Prompt:

How do shared experiences of both joy and sorrow strengthen the
bond in a relationship?

Supplementary Content:

The Latin phrase "Manu in manu" (hand in hand) emphasizes the
partnership and support that come from walking through life
together. The translation seeks to maintain the balance between life's
highs and lows as unified by love.

April 28th

Love

Haiku in English:
In each other's arms,
We find solace and comfort,
Heartbeats synchronized.

Latin Translation:
In alterius complexu,
Solacium et confortium invenimus,
Cordis pulsus congruunt.

Reflection Prompt:

Think about the physical and emotional comfort that comes from being in the embrace of a loved one. How does this connection manifest in everyday life?

Supplementary Content:

"Complexu" (embrace) and "cordis pulsus congruunt" (heartbeats synchronized) highlight the physical closeness and emotional harmony that define intimate relationships.

April 29th

Love

Haiku in English:
Through stormy nights,
Your embrace is my safe haven,
Love's shelter holds strong.

Latin Translation:
Per noctes tempestosas,
Complexus tuus refugium meum est,
Amoris protectio valida.

Reflection Prompt:

Reflect on how love provides a sense of safety and protection during challenging times. How does this shelter help you weather life's storms?

Supplementary Content:

"Refugium meum" (my safe haven) and "amoris protectio valida" (love's strong protection) convey the security and strength found in a loving embrace during difficult moments.

April 30th

Love

Haiku in English:
Shared laughter echoes,
Filling our home with pure joy,
Together we thrive.

Latin Translation:
Risus communis resonat,
Domum nostram laetitia pura implet,
Una prosperamus.

Reflection Prompt:

Consider the role of laughter in a relationship. How does it contribute to the sense of home and togetherness?

Supplementary Content:

"Risus communis" (shared laughter) and "una prosperamus" (together we thrive) emphasize the joy and unity brought about by moments of shared happiness and laughter.

May 1st

Love

Haiku in English:
In silent whispers,
Our hearts speak volumes of love,
Connection runs deep.

Latin Translation:
In susurris tacitis,
Corda nostra de amore multa loquuntur,
Connexio profunda est.

Reflection Prompt:

How can silent moments and whispers convey more than spoken words? Reflect on the depth of connection that silent communication can bring.

Supplementary Content:

"Corda nostra de amore multa loquuntur" (our hearts speak volumes of love) captures the powerful and often unspoken communication that deepens connections in relationships.

May 2nd

Love

Haiku in English:
Life's burdens shared,
Halved by our mutual trust,
Strength in unity.

Latin Translation:
Onera vitae communia,
Mutua fide dimidia,
Robur in unitate.

Reflection Prompt:

Reflect on how sharing life's burdens with a trusted partner can lighten the load. How does mutual trust contribute to the strength of a relationship?

Supplementary Content:

"Onera vitae communia" (life's shared burdens) and "mutua fide dimidia" (halved by mutual trust) emphasize the power of collaboration and trust in navigating life's challenges.

May 3rd

Love

Haiku in English:
Eyes meeting softly,
A universe in your gaze,
Love's eternal dance.

Latin Translation:
Oculi leniter conveniunt,
Universum in tuo aspectu,
Aeterna saltatio amoris.

Reflection Prompt:

Consider the significance of eye contact in conveying deep emotions. How does a shared gaze communicate a universe of feelings?

Supplementary Content:

"Universum in tuo aspectu" (a universe in your gaze) and "aeterna saltatio amoris" (love's eternal dance) highlight the profound connection and timelessness conveyed through eye contact.

May 4th

Love

Haiku in English:
Through every trial,
Your love remains my anchor,
Steadfast and constant.

Latin Translation:
Per omnia tentamina,
Amor tuus anchoram meam manet,
Stabilis et constans.

Reflection Prompt:

Reflect on how love serves as an anchor during difficult times. How does this steadfastness provide stability and comfort?

Supplementary Content:

"Amor tuus anchoram meam manet" (your love remains my anchor) emphasizes the unwavering support and stability that love offers in times of trial.

May 5th

Love

Haiku in English:
Moments of pure bliss,
Found in your tender presence,
Hearts intertwined.

Latin Translation:
Momenta purae beatitudinis,
In tua tenera praesentia inventa,
Corda intertexta.

Reflection Prompt:

Think about the moments of pure happiness experienced with a loved one. How do these moments shape the relationship?

Supplementary Content:

"Tenera praesentia" (tender presence) and "corda intertexta" (hearts intertwined) highlight the deep emotional bond and joy found in each other's company.

May 6th

Love
Haiku in English:
Side by side we grow,
In love's garden, we flourish,
Blooming hand in hand.

Latin Translation:
Latus ad latus crescimus,
In horto amoris, floremus,
Manu in manu florescentes.

Reflection Prompt:

Reflect on the metaphor of a garden for a relationship. How does nurturing and growth together lead to flourishing love?

Supplementary Content:

"In horto amoris" (in love's garden) and "manu in manu florescentes" (blooming hand in hand) evoke the imagery of mutual growth and flourishing within a loving relationship.

May 7th

Love

Haiku in English:
Through joy and sorrow,
Your love is my guiding light,
Eternal and true.

Latin Translation:
Per gaudium et dolorem,
Amor tuus lucerna mea est,
Aeternus et verus.

Reflection Prompt:

Consider the role of love as a guiding light in both joyful and sorrowful times. How does this eternal presence shape your journey together?

Supplementary Content:

"Amor tuus lucerna mea est" (your love is my guiding light) and "aeternus et verus" (eternal and true) emphasize the enduring and faithful nature of love as a constant guide.

May 8th

Love

Haiku in English:
In life's quiet times,
We find peace in each other,
Love's sweet sanctuary.

Latin Translation:
In temporibus quietis vitae,
Pacem in invicem invenimus,
Dulce amoris sanctuarium.

Reflection Prompt:

Reflect on the importance of quiet moments together. How do these moments of peace contribute to the sanctuary of love?

Supplementary Content:

"Dulce amoris sanctuarium" (love's sweet sanctuary) highlights the peaceful and safe haven that love provides during the quiet times of life.

May 9th

Love

Haiku in English:
Gentle hands caress,
Whispers shared in twilight's glow,
Hearts find peace in love.

Latin Translation:
Mites manus tangunt,
Susurri in crepusculo,
Corda pacem in amore inveniunt.

Reflection Prompt:

How does physical touch contribute to feelings of peace and connection in relationships?

Supplementary Content:

The translation captures the intimacy of "gentle hands" with "mites manus" and maintains the delicate imagery of whispers in the twilight.

May 10th

Love

Haiku in English:
Eyes meet in silence,
A world unfolds in a glance,
Love's silent promise.

Latin Translation:
Oculi in silentio conveniunt,
Mundus in aspectu aperitur,
Amoris tacita promissio.

Reflection Prompt:

What can be communicated through a glance that words may not convey? How does this shape our understanding of love's silent promises?

Supplementary Content:

"Amoris tacita promissio" (love's silent promise) conveys the unspoken bond and deep connection that can exist between two people.

May 11th

Love

Haiku in English:
Love's warm embrace holds,
In the stillness of the night,
Two souls intertwined.

Latin Translation:
Amoris calor tenet,
In noctis quiete,
Duae animae intertextae.

Reflection Prompt:

Reflect on the significance of quiet moments in a relationship. How do these moments contribute to the feeling of being intertwined with another soul?

Supplementary Content:

"Duae animae intertextae" (two souls intertwined) beautifully illustrates the deep connection and unity felt in moments of stillness.

May 12th

Love
Haiku in English:
Soft laughter shared late,
Candles flicker in moonlight,
Love's gentle whisper.

Latin Translation:
Risus mitis tarde,
Candelae sub luce lunae tremunt,
Amoris susurrus lenis.

Reflection Prompt:

How does sharing laughter contribute to the intimacy and strength of a relationship?

Supplementary Content:

"Amoris susurrus lenis" (love's gentle whisper) captures the delicate and soothing nature of love communicated in quiet, intimate moments.

May 13th

Love

Haiku in English:
Morning sun brings light,
Love's kiss awakens the heart,
Day begins with joy.

Latin Translation:
Sol matutinus lucem affert,
Amoris osculum cor excitat,
Dies gaudio incipit.

Reflection Prompt:

Consider the symbolism of morning and a new day in the context of love. How do new beginnings enhance our relationships?

Supplementary Content:

The translation retains the freshness and positivity of the morning sun and love's kiss, reflecting the renewal and joy they bring.

May 14th

Love

Haiku in English:
Through life's ups and downs,
Love's steady hand guides the way,
Hearts remain as one.

Latin Translation:
Per vitae altitudines et dejectiones,
Amoris manus firma viam ducit,
Corda ut unum manent.

Reflection Prompt:

How does a steady and reliable presence in love help navigate the challenges of life?

Supplementary Content:

"Amoris manus firma" (love's steady hand) emphasizes the guiding and stabilizing role love plays in our lives, especially during difficult times.

May 15th

Love

Haiku in English:
Rain taps on windows,
Love's warmth shields from the cold storm,
Together we thrive.

Latin Translation:
Pluvia in fenestras pulsans,
Amoris calor a frigore defendit,
Una prosperamus.

Reflection Prompt:

Reflect on how love provides comfort and protection during difficult times. How does this support enable growth and thriving together?

Supplementary Content:

"Amoris calor a frigore defendit" (love's warmth shields from the cold) conveys the comforting and protective nature of love amidst life's storms.

May 16th

Love

Haiku in English:
Under starry skies,
Love's dreams whisper sweet and soft,
Eternal starlight.

Latin Translation:
Sub stellatis caelis,
Amoris somnia dulcia et mollia susurrant,
Aeterna lux stellarum.

Reflection Prompt:

What do starry skies symbolize in the context of love and dreams?
How does the imagery of eternity enhance the theme of lasting love?

Supplementary Content:

"Aeterna lux stellarum" (eternal starlight) captures the timeless and
enduring nature of love's dreams and aspirations.

May 17th

Love

Haiku in English:
Love's melody plays,
Hearts beat in perfect rhythm,
Life's dance begins here.

Latin Translation:
Amoris melodia canit,
Corda in perfecta rhythmo pulsant,
Saltatio vitae hic incipit.

Reflection Prompt:

Consider how love's rhythm and melody influence the "dance" of life. How do harmony and synchronization play a role in relationships?

Supplementary Content:

"Corda in perfecta rhythmo" (hearts in perfect rhythm) illustrates the harmonious and coordinated nature of love that drives the dance of life.

May 18th

Love

Haiku in English:
Love's light never dims,
In the darkest nights it shines,
Guiding us always.

Latin Translation:
Lux amoris numquam obscuratur,
In obscurissimis noctibus splendet,
Semper nos ducens.

Reflection Prompt:

How does love act as a guiding light during difficult times? Reflect on the enduring and unwavering nature of love.

Supplementary Content:

"Lux amoris numquam obscuratur" (love's light never dims) emphasizes the constant and reliable presence of love, even in the darkest moments.

May 19th

Love

Haiku in English:
Love's tender embrace,
In each moment felt anew,
Timeless and profound.

Latin Translation:
Amoris amplexus tener,
In omni momento novus sentitur,
Aeternus et profundus.

Reflection Prompt:

What makes love feel new and profound in each moment? Reflect on the timeless quality of love and how it evolves over time.

Supplementary Content:

"In omni momento novus sentitur" (felt anew in each moment) highlights the refreshing and ever-evolving nature of love's embrace.

May 20th

Love

Haiku in English:
Heartbeats close in tune,
Love's harmony fills the air,
Music of our lives.

Latin Translation:
Cordis pulsus concordes,
Harmonia amoris aerem implet,
Musica vitae nostrae.

Reflection Prompt:

How does the metaphor of music enhance our understanding of love and life? Reflect on the harmony and rhythm found in relationships.

Supplementary Content:

"Harmonia amoris" (love's harmony) and "musica vitae nostrae" (music of our lives) draw a parallel between love and music, illustrating their intertwined and harmonious nature.

May 21st

Love

Haiku in English:
Love's gentle caress,
Moonlight paints a silver dream,
Night of purest peace.

Latin Translation:
Tactus lenis amoris,
Lumen lunae argentum somnium pingit,
Nox purissimae pacis.

Reflection Prompt:

What does moonlight symbolize in the context of love and peace? How do gentle caresses contribute to the serenity of a moment?

Supplementary Content:

"Lumen lunae argentum somnium pingit" (moonlight paints a silver dream) captures the serene and dreamy quality of a peaceful night touched by love.

May 22nd

Love

Haiku in English:
In love's soft shelter,
We find solace and comfort,
Heart to heart we speak.

Latin Translation:
In amore leni refugio,
Solacium et confortium invenimus,
Cor ad cor loquimur.

Reflection Prompt:

Reflect on the concept of love as a shelter. How does it provide solace and comfort, and how does it facilitate deeper communication?

Supplementary Content:

"In amore leni refugio" (in love's soft shelter) underscores the protective and nurturing aspect of love that fosters intimacy and open communication.

May 23rd

Love

Haiku in English:
Love's journey begins,
With every step, hearts align,
Forever entwined.

Latin Translation:
Iter amoris incipit,
Omni gradu, corda coniunguntur,
Aeternum intertexta.

Reflection Prompt:

Consider the metaphor of a journey for love. How do shared steps and aligned hearts contribute to a lasting and intertwined relationship?

Supplementary Content:

"Iter amoris incipit" (love's journey begins) and "aeternum intertexta" (forever entwined) evoke the sense of a shared, enduring path filled with unity and connection.

May 24th

Morality and conscience

Haiku in English:
Cold steel, endless war,
Compassion fades in the dark,
Victory's hollow.

Latin Translation:
Ferrum frigidum, bellum sine fine,
Misericordia in tenebris evanescit,
Victoria vacua.

Reflection Prompt:

What does "victory" mean in a world without compassion? Can true success be achieved without empathy?

Supplementary Content:

Translating "compassion" to "misericordia" captures the sense of mercy and kindness that fades in the darkness of war, illustrating the poem's theme of hollow triumph.

May 25th

Morality and conscience
Haiku in English:
Shadows claim the heart,
Humanity is lost,
Triumph without soul.

Latin Translation:
Umbrae cor occupant,
Humanitas perit,
Triumphus sine anima.

Reflection Prompt:
How do the "shadows" symbolize the loss of humanity? What happens to a society that wins without a soul?

Supplementary Content:
The phrase "sine anima" (without soul) underscores the emptiness of victories achieved through inhuman means, emphasizing the moral cost.

May 26th

Morality and conscience

Haiku in English:
In a void, we fight,
Conscience silenced by the sword,
Empty is the night.

Latin Translation:
In vacuo pugnamus,
Conscientia gladio tacita,
Nox vacua est.

Reflection Prompt:

Consider the impact of a silenced conscience. How does this shape the nature of conflict and its outcomes?

Supplementary Content:

The Latin "Conscientia gladio tacita" (conscience silenced by the sword) vividly conveys the theme of moral suppression in battle.

May 27th

Morality and conscience
Haiku in English:
Power's ruthless grip,
Mercy abandoned, cold,
Dominance reigns king.

Latin Translation:
Potestatis ferox manus,
Misericordia relicta, frigida,
Dominatus regnat rex.

Reflection Prompt:

Reflect on the cost of abandoning mercy for power. How does this affect the ruler and the ruled?

Supplementary Content:

"Potestatis ferox manus" (power's ruthless grip) reflects the harsh control and lack of compassion in a dominion-focused society.

May 28th

Morality and conscience

Haiku in English:
No love, only might,
Hearts turned to stone, ice within,
Triumph cold and stark.

Latin Translation:
Non amor, solum vis,
Corda in lapides versa, intus glacies,
Triumphus frigidus et asper.

Reflection Prompt:

What is the significance of a "heart turned to stone"? How does this imagery relate to the concept of a cold triumph?

Supplementary Content:

The transformation of "corda" (hearts) into "lapides" (stones) highlights the emotional desolation that accompanies a victory devoid of love.

May 29th

Morality and conscience

Haiku in English:
Ethics cast aside,
Injustice rules over all,
Humanity's fall.

Latin Translation:
Ethica neglecta,
Iniquitas super omnia regnat,
Humanitatis casus.

Reflection Prompt:

Discuss the consequences of neglecting ethics. How does injustice lead to the downfall of humanity?

Supplementary Content:

"Ethica neglecta" (ethics cast aside) and "Iniquitas super omnia regnat" (injustice rules over all) together paint a picture of moral decay.

May 30th

Morality and conscience

Haiku in English:
Victory's dark prize,
Empathy nowhere to find,
Souls in shadows hide.

Latin Translation:
Victoriae praemium obscurum,
Empathia nusquam reperienda,
Animae in umbris latent.

Reflection Prompt:

Consider the phrase "souls in shadows hide." What does this say about the personal cost of a dark victory?

Supplementary Content:

The use of "obscurum" (dark) and "umbriae" (shadows) enhances the imagery of a triumph that brings darkness rather than light.

May 31st

Morality and conscience
Haiku in English:
Struggle without end,
Morality fades to dust,
Cold dominion stands.

Latin Translation:
Certamen sine fine,
Moralitatis pulvis evanescit,
Frigidus dominium manet.

Reflection Prompt:

What does it mean for morality to fade to dust? How does this imagery affect our understanding of endless struggle?

Supplementary Content:

"Moralitatis pulvis evanescit" (morality fades to dust) evokes the erosion of ethical values over prolonged conflict.

June 1st

Morality and conscience

Haiku in English:
Conscience lies in chains,
Victory's song echoes harsh,
Humanity wanes.

Latin Translation:
Conscientia in catenis iacet,
Victoriae cantus aspere resonat,
Humanitas decrescit.

Reflection Prompt:

Reflect on the image of a chained conscience. How does this shape the harshness of victory's song?

Supplementary Content:

"Conscientia in catenis" (conscience in chains) poignantly illustrates the suppression of moral judgment in the pursuit of victory.

June 2nd

Morality and conscience

Haiku in English:
Souls bereft of light,
In a world of endless night,
Triumph brings no peace.

Latin Translation:
Animae luce orbae,
In mundo noctis perpetuae,
Triumphus pacem non affert.

Reflection Prompt:

What is the significance of a "world of endless night"? How does this setting influence the nature of triumph?

Supplementary Content:

"Animae luce orbae" (souls bereft of light) emphasizes the spiritual and emotional darkness prevailing in a world without peace.

June 3rd

Morality and conscience
Haiku in English:
Honor fades away,
Power's grip tightens its hold,
Hearts grow cold as stone.

Latin Translation:
Honor evanescit,
Potestatis manus stringit,
Corda ut lapis frigidiora.

Reflection Prompt:

Discuss the interplay between fading honor and the tightening grip of power. How does this affect the human heart?

Supplementary Content:

"Honor evanescit" (honor fades) and "Potestatis manus stringit" (power's grip tightens) together show the inverse relationship between ethical values and control.

June 4th

Morality and conscience

Haiku in English:
No moral compass,
Directionless, we wander,
Victory's cruel cost.

Latin Translation:
Sine compasso morali,
Sine directione, erramus,
Crudelis victoriae sumptus.

Reflection Prompt:

What are the dangers of lacking a moral compass? How does this impact the journey towards victory?

Supplementary Content:

"Sine compasso morali" (without a moral compass) and "erramus" (we wander) depict a society lost and aimless, illustrating the dire consequences.

June 5th

Morality and conscience

Haiku in English:
In the struggle's heat,
Humanity is scorched,
Victory is bleak.

Latin Translation:
In ardore certaminis,
Humanitas aduritur,
Victoria tristis est.

Reflection Prompt:

Consider the imagery of humanity being scorched. How does this reflect the poem's view on the nature of struggle and victory?

Supplementary Content:

"In ardore certaminis" (in the struggle's heat) conveys the intense and damaging impact of prolonged conflict on human values.

June 6th

Morality and conscience
Haiku in English:
Compassion's last breath,
Struggle's endless cycle spins,
Triumph's empty crown.

Latin Translation:
Ultimus misericordiae spiritus,
Certaminis circulus perpetuus volvitur,
Vacuus victoriae corona.

Reflection Prompt:

What does "compassion's last breath" signify in the context of an endless struggle? How does this impact the value of triumph?

Supplementary Content:

"Ultimus misericordiae spiritus" (compassion's last breath) suggests the final vestiges of empathy being extinguished in relentless conflict.

June 7th

Morality and conscience
Haiku in English:
World void of kindness,
Only might and victory,
Souls lost to the dark.

Latin Translation:
Mundus sine benignitate,
Sola vis et victoria,
Animae tenebris perditae.

Reflection Prompt:

Reflect on the consequences of a world devoid of kindness. How does this shape the nature of might and victory?

Supplementary Content:

"Mundus sine benignitate" (world without kindness) sets the stage for a bleak reality where only power prevails, highlighting the moral cost.

June 8th

Advertising

Haiku in English:
Work till you collapse,
Fashion masks the weary soul,
Ads dictate our worth.

Latin Translation:
Labor donec concidas,
Moda animam fessam celat,
Reclamationes valorem dant.

Reflection Prompt:

Consider how advertisements shape your sense of self-worth. Do they uplift or undermine you?

Supplementary Content:

In translating, "collapse" was rendered as "concidas" to capture the physical and emotional exhaustion implied in the original. The process involved ensuring the tone of weariness was preserved in both languages.

June 9th

Advertising

Haiku in English:
Constant toil, no rest,
Clothes conceal the silent cries,
Brands define our pride.

Latin Translation:
Perpetuus labor, sine requie,
Vestimenta clamores tacitos celant,
Notae superbiam definiunt.

Reflection Prompt:

Think about the role of brands in your life. How do they influence your feelings of pride?

Supplementary Content:

"Perpetuus labor" translates the relentless nature of constant toil. The challenge was to maintain the subtle critique of consumer culture present in the original.

June 10th

Advertising

Haiku in English:
Driven to the edge,
Labels hide the inner void,
Advertisements rule.

Latin Translation:
Ad marginem impulsus,
Tituli vacuum internum celant,
Reclamationes regunt.

Reflection Prompt:

Reflect on how consumer culture impacts your inner sense of fulfillment. Are you driven by external labels?

Supplementary Content:

"Ad marginem impulsus" emphasizes being pushed to the brink, a crucial element in conveying the intensity of the original sentiment.

June 11th

Advertising

Haiku in English:
Exhausted we strive,
Fashion's sheen, a fragile shield,
Told what to desire.

Latin Translation:
Fessi contendimus,
Splendor modae, scutum fragile,
Quid cupiamus dictum est.

Reflection Prompt:

Consider the influence of fashion on your desires. Are these desires truly yours or shaped by external forces?

Supplementary Content:

"Scutum fragile" directly translates to "fragile shield," highlighting the precarious protection fashion offers against deeper issues.

June 12th

Advertising

Haiku in English:
Chasing endless goals,
Garments veil our empty hearts,
Ads feed vanity.

Latin Translation:
Metas sine fine sequimur,
Vestes corda vacua velant,
Reclamationes vanitatem alunt.

Reflection Prompt:

Think about your goals and aspirations. Are they driven by personal ambition or external validation?

Supplementary Content:

"Metas sine fine sequimur" conveys the never-ending pursuit of goals, capturing the essence of endless ambition and its impact on personal fulfillment.

June 13th

Advertising

Haiku in English:
Labors never end,
Clothing masks the hollow mind,
Persuaded by ads.

Latin Translation:
Labor sine fine,
Vestimenta mentem vacuam celant,
Reclamationibus persuasum.

Reflection Prompt:

Reflect on how advertising influences your thoughts and beliefs. How much do you buy into these messages?

Supplementary Content:

"Vestimenta mentem vacuam celant" was chosen to convey the idea of clothing hiding a hollow mind, emphasizing the superficiality of consumerism.

June 14th

Advertising

Haiku in English:
Working non-stop lives,
Fashion hides the inner strife,
Consumer minds bend.

Latin Translation:
Vitae sine intermissione laborantes,
Moda luctum internum celat,
Mentes consumentium flectuntur.

Reflection Prompt:

Consider how continuous work affects your mental health. Do you use fashion to mask these struggles?

Supplementary Content:

"Vitae sine intermissione laborantes" emphasizes non-stop working lives, capturing the relentless pace of modern life and its impact on mental well-being.

June 15th

Advertising

Haiku in English:
Incessant labor,
Stylish facades cover pain,
Ads shape our esteem.

Latin Translation:
Labor incessans,
Facies elegantes dolorem tegunt,
Reclamationes existimationem formant.

Reflection Prompt:

Think about how fashion and advertising shape your self-esteem. Are you presenting a true or curated version of yourself?

Supplementary Content:

"Facies elegantes dolorem tegunt" translates to "stylish facades cover pain," highlighting the superficial nature of fashion in masking deeper emotional issues.

June 16th

Advertising

Haiku in English:
Full capacity,
Designer brands hide the stress,
Marketing controls.

Latin Translation:
Capacitas plena,
Notae designatores anxietatem celant,
Mercatus imperat.

Reflection Prompt:

Reflect on how marketing strategies influence your stress levels. Are you aware of their impact on your life?

Supplementary Content:

"Capacitas plena" emphasizes the idea of working at full capacity, capturing the high demands and stress of modern work life masked by designer brands.

June 17th

Advertising

Haiku in English:
No break in the grind,
Fashion dulls the silent screams,
We believe the ads.

Latin Translation:
Nulla pausa in labore,
Moda clamores tacitos obruit,
Reclamationibus credimus.

Reflection Prompt:

Consider how much you trust advertisements. Do they genuinely address your needs or simply create new ones?

Supplementary Content:

"Moda clamores tacitos obruit" was chosen to convey the idea of fashion dulling silent screams, emphasizing the superficial relief fashion provides against deeper issues.

June 18th

Advertising

Haiku in English:
Striving to the brink,
Clothes obscure the weary soul,
Commercials deceive.

Latin Translation:
Ad limitem contendentes,
Vestes animam fessam celant,
Commercialia decipiunt.

Reflection Prompt:

Think about the impact of commercials on your sense of self. Are they leading you towards or away from your true self?

Supplementary Content:

"Commercialia decipiunt" directly translates to "commercials deceive," capturing the essence of how advertising can mislead and manipulate.

June 19th

Advertising

Haiku in English:
Burnout's hidden face,
Garments cloak the empty chase,
Ads whisper our worth.

Latin Translation:
Vultus burnout celatus,
Vestimenta inane cursum tegunt,
Reclamationes valorem susurrant.

Reflection Prompt:

Reflect on how burnout affects you. Are your achievements masking deeper issues?

Supplementary Content:

"Vultus burnout celatus" highlights the hidden face of burnout, emphasizing how external appearances can conceal internal struggles.

June 20th

Advertising

Haiku in English:
Never-ending work,
Fashion hides the inner hurt,
Media dictates.

Latin Translation:
Labor sine fine,
Moda dolorem internum celat,
Media imperant.

Reflection Prompt:

Consider the role of media in your life. How much influence does it have over your emotions and decisions?

Supplementary Content:

"Media imperant" translates to "media dictates," capturing the pervasive influence of media on personal beliefs and feelings.

June 21st

Advertising

Haiku in English:
Pushed beyond our means,
Stylish fronts conceal despair,
Ads shape self-esteem.

Latin Translation:
Ultra vires nostras impulsi,
Frontes elegantes desperationem tegunt,
Reclamationes existimationem formant.

Reflection Prompt:

Think about how advertisements shape your self-esteem. Are they reinforcing positive or negative self-images?

Supplementary Content:

"Ultra vires nostras impulsi" conveys being pushed beyond one's means, emphasizing the extreme pressures exerted by consumer culture.

June 22nd

Advertising

Haiku in English:
Toil without respite,
Fashion masks the tired heart,
Ads carve out our needs.

Latin Translation:
Labor sine requie,
Moda cor fessum celat,
Reclamationes necessitates formant.

Reflection Prompt:

Reflect on how advertising shapes your perceived needs. Are these needs genuine or manufactured?

Supplementary Content:

"Labor sine requie" translates to "toil without respite," emphasizing the relentless nature of modern work life and its emotional toll.

June 23rd

Passion

Haiku in English:
Fire in our veins,
Lips meet in a fervent kiss,
Bound by lust's sweet chains.

Latin Translation:
Ignis in venis nostris,
Labra in ferventi osculo conveniunt,
Vinculis dulcis libidinis ligati.

Reflection Prompt:

How does the imagery of fire and chains enhance your understanding of passion and desire? Reflect on a time when you felt such intense emotion.

Supplementary Content:

The phrase "Ignis in venis nostris" translates directly to "fire in our veins," capturing the intense and primal nature of the original haiku. Translating the phrase "Bound by lust's sweet chains" required careful selection to maintain the delicate balance between desire and constraint.

June 24th

Passion

Haiku in English:
Hearts beat as one flame,
In the dance of night's embrace,
Love's wild symphony.

Latin Translation:
Corda ut una flamma pulsant,
In saltatione amplexus noctis,
Symphonia fera amoris.

Reflection Prompt:

Think about a moment when your heart felt in sync with someone else's. How does the metaphor of a symphony resonate with your experience of love?

Supplementary Content:

"Corda ut una flamma pulsant" translates to "hearts beat as one flame," vividly portraying the unity and intensity of love. Maintaining the musical metaphor in "Symphonia fera amoris" was crucial to keep the wild and untamed essence of the haiku.

June 25th

Passion

Haiku in English:
Touch ignites the spark,
Whispers turn to heated moans,
Passion's wild embark.

Latin Translation:
Tactus scintillam accendit,
Susurri in gemitus calidos vertuntur,
Initium ferox passionis.

Reflection Prompt:

Consider the power of touch in your relationships. How does physical contact transform emotional intimacy for you?

Supplementary Content:

"Tactus scintillam accendit" translates to "touch ignites the spark," emphasizing the catalytic role of touch in passion. Ensuring the transformation of "whispers to heated moans" captured the escalating intensity in the haiku.

June 26th

Passion

Haiku in English:
Desire's gentle pull,
Skin to skin, we lose control,
In rapture's sweet lull.

Latin Translation:
Trahat lenis cupiditas,
Cutis ad cutem, nos imperium amittimus,
In dulci quiete extasis.

Reflection Prompt:

How does the concept of losing control in moments of intimacy resonate with you? Reflect on the balance between control and surrender in your life.

Supplementary Content:

"Trahat lenis cupiditas" translates to "desire's gentle pull," highlighting the soft yet irresistible nature of desire. Preserving the imagery of "skin to skin" and the sense of losing control was essential to the haiku's impact.

June 27th

Passion

Haiku in English:
Stars fall from the sky,
As we meld in fiery bliss,
Lost in passion's cry.

Latin Translation:
Stellae e caelo cadunt,
Dum in beata flamma coalescimus,
In clamore passionis amissi.

Reflection Prompt:

What emotions do the falling stars symbolize for you? How do moments of intense passion affect your perception of reality?

Supplementary Content:

"Stellae e caelo cadunt" vividly translates to "stars fall from the sky," a powerful image of celestial intensity. Maintaining the fiery bliss and the sense of being "lost in passion's cry" was crucial to the haiku's evocative nature.

June 28th

Passion

Haiku in English:
Breath of the night air,
Entwined in sheer ecstasy,
Love's tender affair.

Latin Translation:
Spiritus nocturni aeris,
In pura extasi intorti,
Teneri amoris negotium.

Reflection Prompt:

Consider the significance of night in your intimate experiences. How does the night air enhance moments of ecstasy and tenderness?

Supplementary Content:

"Spiritus nocturni aeris" translates to "breath of the night air," capturing the tranquil yet potent backdrop of night. Ensuring the entwined ecstasy and tender affair was conveyed accurately was key to preserving the haiku's sensual tone.

June 29th

Passion

Haiku in English:
Gentle, heated touch,
Lovers lost in timeless dance,
Bound in love's sweet clutch.

Latin Translation:
Tactus lenis et calidus,
Amatores in saltatione intempestiva amissi,
In dulci prehensione amoris ligati.

Reflection Prompt:

Think about a time when you felt lost in the moment with a loved one. How does the imagery of a timeless dance relate to your experience of love?

Supplementary Content:

"Tactus lenis et calidus" translates to "gentle, heated touch," balancing the softness and intensity of touch. Capturing the timeless dance and the binding clutch of love was essential to convey the haiku's sense of enduring passion.

June 30th

Passion

Haiku in English:
Eager hands explore,
Secrets whispered in the dark,
Love's endless allure.

Latin Translation:
Manus cupidae explorant,
Arcana in tenebris susurrata,
Interminabilis amoris allectatio.

Reflection Prompt:

How do you feel when you share secrets in intimate moments? Reflect on the allure of discovery in your relationships.

Supplementary Content:

"Manus cupidae explorant" translates to "eager hands explore," capturing the curiosity and desire in intimate moments. Maintaining the whispered secrets and endless allure was key to preserving the haiku's sense of mystery and attraction.

July 1st

Passion

Haiku in English:
Passionate and raw,
Bodies merge in heated bliss,
Breaking every law.

Latin Translation:
Ardens et rudis,
Corpora in beata calore coalescunt,
Omnem legem frangentes.

Reflection Prompt:

Consider the rebellious nature of love and passion. How do you balance societal norms with your personal desires?

Supplementary Content:

"Ardens et rudis" translates to "passionate and raw," highlighting the unrefined intensity of the emotions. Ensuring the merging of bodies and the breaking of laws captured the haiku's sense of defiance and bliss.

July 2nd

Passion
Haiku in English:
Night's embrace so deep,
Silken threads of love entwined,
In passion, we leap.

Latin Translation:
Amplexus noctis tam profundus,
Serica fila amoris intorta,
In passionem, salimus.

Reflection Prompt:

How does the depth of night enhance your feelings of love and passion? Reflect on the metaphor of leaping into passion and what it means to you.

Supplementary Content:

"Amplexus noctis tam profundus" translates to "night's embrace so deep," emphasizing the enveloping nature of night. Capturing the silken threads and the leap into passion was crucial to convey the haiku's sense of immersive love.

July 3rd

Nature

Haiku in English:
Raspberries forgotten,
Bush's sweetness lost to time,
Nature's gift fades fast.

Latin Translation:
Fraga oblita,
Dulcedo rubi perditur,
Naturae donum cito evanescit.

Reflection Prompt:

Think about a time you tasted fresh fruit from the wild. How does the experience of nature's pure flavors differ from store-bought alternatives?

Supplementary Content:

"Fraga oblita" translates to "forgotten raspberries," emphasizing the rapid disappearance of natural sweetness. This haiku captures the fleeting nature of fresh, wild produce compared to cultivated counterparts.

July 4th

Nature

Haiku in English:
Tomatoes once rich,
Intensive farming strips taste,
Flavors lost in haste.

Latin Translation:
Tomacula olim dives,
Agricultura intensiva gustum aufert,
Sapores in festinatione perditi.

Reflection Prompt:

Consider the trade-offs of intensive farming. How can we balance the need for mass production with the preservation of flavor and quality?

Supplementary Content:

"Tomacula olim dives" refers to the once rich flavor of tomatoes. This haiku critiques the consequences of industrial farming practices on the taste and quality of produce.

July 5th

Nature

Haiku in English:
End times we now face,
Black wine berries lost to past,
Nature's taste erased.

Latin Translation:
Finis temporum nunc,
Vini nigri morae praeteritis perditae,
Gustus naturae deletus.

Reflection Prompt:

Reflect on the concept of "end times" in relation to biodiversity. How does the loss of certain plant species impact our cultural and natural heritage?

Supplementary Content:

"Vini nigri morae" highlights the loss of black wine berries, symbolizing the broader erosion of natural flavors and biodiversity in the face of modern challenges.

July 6th

Nature

Haiku in English:
Crown of the hand speaks,
Whispers of eternity,
Forgotten wisdom.

Latin Translation:
Corona manus loquitur,
Susurri aeternitatis,
Sapientia oblita.

Reflection Prompt:

What ancient wisdom have we lost in our pursuit of progress? How can we reconnect with the timeless teachings of nature?

Supplementary Content:

"Corona manus" or "crown of the hand" symbolizes the forgotten wisdom once held in our hands, passed down through generations. This haiku evokes the loss of ancient knowledge and the need to rediscover it.

July 7th

Nature
Haiku in English:
Swallows shyly glide,
Their grace unnoticed by us,
Nature's dance ignored.

Latin Translation:
Hirundines timide volitant,
Gratia eorum a nobis neglecta,
Chorus naturae neglectus.

Reflection Prompt:
Think about a moment when you witnessed the subtle beauty of nature. Why do we often overlook such moments, and how can we become more attuned to them?

Supplementary Content:
"Hirundines timide volitant" captures the shy flight of swallows, a delicate dance often overlooked. This haiku encourages mindfulness and appreciation of nature's understated beauty.

July 8th

Nature

Haiku in English:
Oh blackbird, you sing,
Your melody now a ghost,
Missed in our silence.

Latin Translation:
O merula, cantas,
Tua melodia nunc umbra,
In nostro silentio desiderata.

Reflection Prompt:

Consider the significance of birdsong in your daily life. How does its absence impact our connection to the natural world?

Supplementary Content:

"O merula, cantas" addresses the blackbird's song, now a ghostly memory. This haiku reflects on the fading presence of natural sounds in our environment.

July 9th

Nature

Haiku in English:
Nature's flavors fade,
Heirloom tastes lost in progress,
Memories now pale.

Latin Translation:
Naturae sapores evanescunt,
Gustus antiqui in progressu perditi,
Memoriae nunc pallent.

Reflection Prompt:

How do heirloom varieties of fruits and vegetables differ from modern hybrids? What value do they hold for future generations?

Supplementary Content:

"Naturae sapores evanescunt" highlights the fading flavors of nature. This haiku mourns the loss of heirloom tastes amidst agricultural progress and the pale memories they leave behind.

July 10th

Nature

Haiku in English:
Bush berries once sweet,
Industrial hands steal joy,
Nature's song grows faint.

Latin Translation:
Baccae rubi olim dulces,
Manus industriae gaudium auferunt,
Carmen naturae obscuratur.

Reflection Prompt:

Reflect on the impact of industrial agriculture on local ecosystems and traditional practices. How can we reclaim the joy of natural flavors?

Supplementary Content:

"Baccae rubi olim dulces" refers to once sweet bush berries. This haiku laments the joy stolen by industrialization and the resulting faintness of nature's song.

July 11th

Nature

Haiku in English:
Eternal whispers,
Crown of hand's ancient stories,
Now lost in the noise.

Latin Translation:
Susurri aeterni,
Corona manus antiquis fabulis,
Nunc in strepitu perditi.

Reflection Prompt:

What stories and traditions have been drowned out by modern life? How can we preserve and honor these ancient narratives?

Supplementary Content:

"Corona manus antiquis fabulis" conveys the ancient stories held in our hands. This haiku explores the loss of eternal whispers and wisdom in the cacophony of contemporary life.

July 12th

Nature

Haiku in English:
Swallows shyly pass,
We no longer see their flight,
Beauty slips away.

Latin Translation:
Hirundines timide transeunt,
Non iam eorum volatum videmus,
Pulchritudo aufugit.

Reflection Prompt:

Think about the fleeting moments of beauty in your surroundings. Why do they often go unnoticed, and how can we become more present to appreciate them?

Supplementary Content:

"Hirundines timide transeunt" describes the shy passing of swallows. This haiku reflects on the unnoticed beauty of nature slipping away from our distracted lives.

July 13th

Nature

Haiku in English:
Blackbird's song now gone,
Nature's voice grows ever faint,
Yearning fills our hearts.

Latin Translation:
Merulae cantus nunc abiit,
Vox naturae semper obscuratur,
Desiderium corda nostra implet.

Reflection Prompt:

How does the disappearance of natural sounds affect our emotional well-being? What can we do to restore these voices?

Supplementary Content:

"Vox naturae semper obscuratur" highlights the ever-fading voice of nature. This haiku expresses the deep yearning in our hearts for the lost melodies of the natural world.

July 14th

Nature

Haiku in English:
Forgotten flavors,
End times of our disconnection,
Nature's call ignored.

Latin Translation:
Gustus obliti,
Finis temporum nostrae disjunctionis,
Vocem naturae neglecta.

Reflection Prompt:

Consider the implications of our disconnection from nature's flavors and rhythms. How can we reestablish a harmonious relationship with the natural world?

Supplementary Content:

"Finis temporum nostrae disjunctionis" signifies the end times of our disconnection. This haiku underscores the ignored call of nature and the forgotten flavors that once connected us.

July 15th

Intimacy

Haiku in English:
Craving touch and sighs,
Bodies merge in fervent dance,
Love's sweet melody.

Latin Translation:
Tactus et suspiria,
Corpora in ardentis saltatione confluunt,
Dulcis melodia amoris.

Reflection Prompt:

How does the imagery of merging bodies and a fervent dance resonate with your own experiences of intimacy? Reflect on the connection between physical touch and emotional connection.

Supplementary Content:

The translation "Tactus et suspiria" captures the delicate balance between the desire for touch and the act of sighing. The Latin phrase "Dulcis melodia amoris" aims to convey the harmonious nature of love as described in the original haiku.

July 16th

Intimacy

Haiku in English:
Lips on fire ignite,
Hearts ablaze in deep desire,
Pleasure's tender light.

Latin Translation:
Labra igne succensa,
Corda ardent in desiderio profundo,
Lux tenera voluptatis.

Reflection Prompt:

Think about a moment when a kiss sparked intense emotions. How do the metaphors of fire and light help illustrate the nature of desire and pleasure?

Supplementary Content:

"Labra igne succensa" translates to "lips on fire ignite," effectively capturing the intense, almost primal reaction described. The phrase "Lux tenera voluptatis" translates to "pleasure's tender light," maintaining the gentle yet powerful impact of desire.

July 17th

Intimacy

Haiku in English:
Breathless whispers meet,
Souls entwined in passion's heat,
Love's timeless retreat.

Latin Translation:
Susurri sine spiritu conveniunt,
Animae in calore passionis implicatae,
Amoris refugium aeternum.

Reflection Prompt:

How does the concept of a "timeless retreat" in love apply to your experiences? Reflect on moments where time seemed to stand still due to emotional intensity.

Supplementary Content:

"Susurri sine spiritu conveniunt" captures the intimate moment of breathless whispers meeting. The translation aims to maintain the original haiku's sense of timelessness and eternal refuge in love.

July 18th

Intimacy

Haiku in English:
Moans in twilight's hush,
Bodies tremble, spirits rush,
Ecstasy's sweet blush.

Latin Translation:
Gemitus in silentio crepusculi,
Corpora tremunt, spiritus festinant,
Dulcis rubor extasis.

Reflection Prompt:

Consider the emotional and physical reactions described in this haiku. How do you experience the balance of calm and intensity in intimate moments?

Supplementary Content:

"Gemitus in silentio crepusculi" translates to "moans in twilight's hush," effectively setting the scene of quiet intensity. The Latin translation aims to preserve the juxtaposition of trembling bodies and rushing spirits.

July 19th

Intimacy
Haiku in English:
Gentle caress glows,
Souls ablaze in tender throes,
Love's eternal prose.

Latin Translation:
Tactus lenis micat,
Animae in dolcibus angustiis ardentes,
Amoris aeterni prosa.

Reflection Prompt:

Reflect on the idea of love being described as "eternal prose." How do your own experiences of love and tenderness compare to the imagery in this haiku?

Supplementary Content:

"Tactus lenis micat" captures the glowing effect of a gentle caress. The translation maintains the haiku's depiction of love's enduring and poetic nature.

July 20th

Intimacy

Haiku in English:
Whispers of delight,
Bodies sway in passion's flight,
Love's ecstatic height.

Latin Translation:
Susurri gaudii,
Corpora in volatu passionis nutant,
Amoris extaticus vertex.

Reflection Prompt:

How does the imagery of bodies swaying in passion reflect your own experiences? Think about the connection between physical movement and emotional elevation.

Supplementary Content:

"Susurri gaudii" translates to "whispers of delight," emphasizing the joyful and intimate nature of the moment. The phrase "Amoris extaticus vertex" aims to convey the peak of love's ecstasy.

July 21st

Intimacy

Haiku in English:
Silk against warm skin,
Shivers ripple deep within,
Pleasure's gentle spin.

Latin Translation:
Serica contra cutem calidam,
Frigores intus profunde vibrantes,
Dulcis voluta voluptatis.

Reflection Prompt:

Consider the sensory experiences described in this haiku. How does the feel of different textures on your skin influence your perception of pleasure and intimacy?

Supplementary Content:

"Serica contra cutem calidam" captures the tactile sensation of silk against warm skin. The translation strives to maintain the depth and nuance of the original haiku's sensory details.

July 22nd

Intimacy

Haiku in English:
Eyes meet in the dark,
Hearts race, bodies entwine,
Passion's fiery spark.

Latin Translation:
Oculi in tenebris conveniunt,
Corda cursitant, corpora intorquentur,
Ignis passionis accenditur.

Reflection Prompt:

Think about the role of eye contact in moments of intimacy. How does the connection of gazes enhance the emotional and physical experience described in this haiku?

Supplementary Content:

"Oculi in tenebris conveniunt" translates to "eyes meet in the dark," emphasizing the connection through gaze. The phrase "Ignis passionis accenditur" captures the ignition of passion described in the haiku.

July 23rd

Intimacy

Haiku in English:
Sighs of longing sigh,
Love's embrace beneath the sky,
Desire's soft reply.

Latin Translation:
Suspiria desiderii,
Amoris complexus sub caelo,
Responsum suave cupiditatis.

Reflection Prompt:

Reflect on the significance of open skies in moments of intimacy. How does nature influence your experiences of love and desire?

Supplementary Content:

"Suspiria desiderii" translates to "sighs of longing," capturing the deep sense of yearning. The translation aims to maintain the openness and softness conveyed in the original haiku.

July 24th

Intimacy

Haiku in English:
Soft whispers echo,
Bodies yearn in tender flow,
Love's purest crescendo.

Latin Translation:
Susurri molles resonant,
Corpora in leni fluxu ardent,
Amoris purissimum crescendo.

Reflection Prompt:

How do whispers and soft voices contribute to moments of intimacy for you? Reflect on the crescendo of emotions and physical sensations in your experiences of love.

Supplementary Content:

"Susurri molles resonant" translates to "soft whispers echo," capturing the gentle yet pervasive nature of intimate communication. The translation strives to maintain the purity and buildup of emotions described in the haiku.

July 25th

Connection

Haiku in English:
Fingers trace desires,
Skin aflame with fervent need,
Pleasure's sweet embrace.

Latin Translation:
Digiti desideria trahunt,
Cutis ardente necessitate flagrans,
Dulcis voluptatis complexus.

Reflection Prompt:

Consider the tactile sensations described. How do touch and the feeling of skin contribute to your experiences of desire and pleasure?

Supplementary Content:

"Digiti desideria trahunt" translates to "fingers trace desires," capturing the intimate act of touch. The translation maintains the fervent need and the sweet embrace described in the original haiku.

July 26th

Connection

Haiku in English:
Breathless ecstasy,
Souls collide in fiery dance,
Hearts beat as one flame.

Latin Translation:
Extasis sine spiritu,
Animae in ignea saltatione colliduntur,
Corda ut una flamma pulsant.

Reflection Prompt:

Think about a time when your emotions and physical sensations were in perfect harmony. How does the imagery of a fiery dance and unified heartbeat resonate with your experiences?

Supplementary Content:

"Extasis sine spiritu" captures the breathless nature of ecstasy. The phrase "Corda ut una flamma pulsant" effectively translates the idea of hearts beating as one flame, emphasizing unity and intensity.

July 27th

Connection

Haiku in English:
Moans in the dark night,
Love's symphony echoes deep,
Bodies intertwined.

Latin Translation:
Gemitus in nocte obscura,
Symphonia amoris resonat altius,
Corpora intorta.

Reflection Prompt:

Reflect on how sounds and echoes can enhance the feeling of intimacy. How does the concept of a symphony relate to the shared experiences of love and connection?

Supplementary Content:

"Gemitus in nocte obscura" translates to "moans in the dark night," setting a scene of deep intimacy. The Latin translation preserves the musicality and depth of the original haiku.

July 28th

Connection

Haiku in English:
Tender lips explore,
Lost in passion's sweet embrace,
Love's soft whispers fade.

Latin Translation:
Labra lenia explorant,
In dulci complexu passionis amissi,
Susurri molles amoris evanescunt.

Reflection Prompt:

Consider the transient nature of passion described in this haiku. How do fleeting moments of intimacy impact your overall experience of love?

Supplementary Content:

"Labra lenia explorant" captures the gentle exploration by lips. The translation aims to maintain the idea of getting lost in passion and the eventual fading of love's whispers.

July 29th

Connection
Haiku in English:
Heat rises within,
Hearts collide in wild embrace,
Desire's fervent cry.

Latin Translation:
Calor intus surgit,
Corda in fera complexione colliduntur,
Ardens cupiditatis clamor.

Reflection Prompt:

Think about how internal heat and external contact influence your feelings of desire. How does the imagery of a wild embrace and fervent cry relate to your experiences?

Supplementary Content:

"Calor intus surgit" translates to "heat rises within," capturing the internal build-up of desire. The phrase "Ardens cupiditatis clamor" emphasizes the intensity and loudness of passion's expression.

July 30th

Connection

Haiku in English:
Sighs in the moonlight,
Shadows dance in tender grace,
Pleasure's gentle sigh.

Latin Translation:
Suspiria in luna,
Umbrarum saltatio in leni gratia,
Dulcis gemitus voluptatis.

Reflection Prompt:

Reflect on how moonlight and shadows create a unique ambiance for intimacy. How do light and shadow play a role in your experiences of pleasure?

Supplementary Content:

"Suspiria in luna" captures the sighs under moonlight, setting a serene scene. The Latin translation maintains the interplay of shadows and tender movements described in the haiku.

July 31st

Connection

Haiku in English:
Whispers in the dark,
Bodies meld in fiery bliss,
Lost in love's embrace.

Latin Translation:
Susurri in tenebris,
Corpora in flamma beata coalescunt,
Amoris complexu amissi.

Reflection Prompt:

Consider the role of darkness and whispers in creating intimate moments. How does the idea of being lost in an embrace resonate with your feelings of love?

Supplementary Content:

"Susurri in tenebris" translates to "whispers in the dark," emphasizing the quiet yet intense nature of the scene. The translation strives to maintain the blissful and enveloping nature of the embrace.

August 1st

Connection
Haiku in English:
Skin on skin we meet,
Passion's fire burns so sweet,
Hearts and souls complete.

Latin Translation:
Cutis ad cutem convenimus,
Ignis passionis tam dulcis ardet,
Corda et animae completae.

Reflection Prompt:

Think about how physical contact enhances emotional connection. How does the imagery of burning sweetly relate to your experiences of passion?

Supplementary Content:

"Cutis ad cutem convenimus" captures the meeting of skin on skin, highlighting physical closeness. The phrase "Corda et animae completae" emphasizes the completion of hearts and souls, preserving the haiku's sense of unity.

August 2nd

Connection

Haiku in English:
Midnight's tender touch,
Hearts entwine in love's embrace,
Ecstasy unfolds.

Latin Translation:
Tactus lenis media nocte,
Corda in amplexu amoris nectuntur,
Extasis explicatur.

Reflection Prompt:

Reflect on how the timing of midnight adds to the feeling of intimacy. How does the idea of ecstasy unfolding resonate with your experiences of deep connection?

Supplementary Content:

"Tactus lenis media nocte" translates to "midnight's tender touch," emphasizing the gentle and timely nature of the scene. The translation maintains the unfolding nature of ecstasy described in the haiku.

August 3rd

Ecstasy

Haiku in English:
Ecstasy's embrace,
Bodies dance in moonlit dreams,
Pleasure's whispered song.

Latin Translation:
Extasis amplexus,
Corpora in somniis lunatis saltant,
Voluptatis carmen susurratum.

Reflection Prompt:

How does the image of "moonlit dreams" affect your perception of intimacy in this haiku? Reflect on a moment when a dream or fantasy influenced your real-life emotions or experiences.

Supplementary Content:

The phrase "somniis lunatis" captures the dreamlike quality of moonlit moments. Translating "Pleasure's whispered song" to "Voluptatis carmen susurratum" emphasizes the delicate and secretive nature of intimate pleasures.

August 4th

Ecstasy

Ecstasy
Haiku in English:
Heat of passion's fire,
Skin on skin, we lose ourselves,
In love's wild tempest.

Latin Translation:
Calor ignis passionis,
Cutis ad cutem, nos amittimus,
In tempestate amoris fera.

Reflection Prompt:

Consider the metaphor of a "wild tempest" in relation to love. How do intense emotions and physical sensations interplay in your experiences of passion?

Supplementary Content:

"Tempestate amoris fera" translates to "wild tempest of love," highlighting the uncontrollable and intense nature of passionate experiences. The translation aims to retain the vivid imagery of skin-to-skin contact and the overwhelming heat of desire.

August 5th

Ecstasy
Haiku in English:
Gentle bites and moans,
Euphoria's sweet descent,
Nights of endless bliss.

Latin Translation:
Morsus lenes et gemitus,
Euphoriae dulcis descensus,
Noctes beatitudinis sine fine.

Reflection Prompt:

Think about how gentle actions like bites and moans contribute to your feelings of euphoria. How do such sensory experiences shape your memories of intimate nights?

Supplementary Content:

"Euphoriae dulcis descensus" captures the gradual and sweet descent into euphoria. The translation preserves the balance between the gentle and intense elements of the original haiku.

August 6th

Ecstasy

Ecstasy

Haiku in English:
Silk sheets, tangled limbs,
Breathless in the throes of love,
Hearts beat fierce and fast.

Latin Translation:
Lintea serica, artus implicati,
Sine spiritu in aestu amoris,
Cordibus ferociter et celeriter pulsat.

Reflection Prompt:

Consider the physical sensations described, such as silk sheets and tangled limbs. How do these details enhance the depiction of passionate encounters in your mind?

Supplementary Content:

"Lintea serica, artus implicati" translates to "silk sheets, tangled limbs," capturing the tactile and intertwined nature of the scene. The Latin version aims to retain the breathless and fierce intensity of love's throes.

August 7th

Ecstasy

Haiku in English:
Whispered promises,
Ecstatic waves wash over,
Together, we soar.

Latin Translation:
Promissa susurrata,
Undae extaticae pervadunt,
Una, ad caelum volamus.

Reflection Prompt:

Think about the role of promises in intimate relationships. How do whispered assurances and shared moments of ecstasy contribute to your sense of connection and trust?

Supplementary Content:

"Promissa susurrata" emphasizes the intimacy and secrecy of whispered promises. The translation aims to convey the shared experience of ecstasy and the feeling of soaring together, enhancing the original haiku's sense of unity.

August 8th

Ecstasy

Haiku in English:
Eyes locked, souls entwined,
Passion's fervor, wild and pure,
Lost in each other.

Latin Translation:
Oculi coniuncti, animae nectuntur,
Ardor passionis, ferox et purus,
In alterutro amissi.

Reflection Prompt:

Reflect on how eye contact can deepen emotional connections. How do intense gazes and the feeling of being "lost in each other" resonate with your experiences of passion and love?

Supplementary Content:

"Oculi coniuncti, animae nectuntur" translates to "eyes locked, souls entwined," highlighting the deep connection formed through eye contact. The translation maintains the balance between wild and pure passion.

August 9th

Ecstasy

Haiku in English:
Midnight's secret kiss,
Hands explore with tender grace,
Pleasure's silent cry.

Latin Translation:
Osculum secretum mediae noctis,
Manus leni gratia explorant,
Clamor tacitus voluptatis.

Reflection Prompt:

Consider the significance of secrecy and tenderness in intimate moments. How do these elements shape your experiences of passion and pleasure?

Supplementary Content:

"Osculum secretum mediae noctis" captures the clandestine nature of a midnight kiss. The translation aims to retain the tender and exploratory nature of the haiku, emphasizing the silent yet powerful expression of pleasure.

August 10th

Ecstasy
Haiku in English:
Heat rises within,
Hearts collide in lustful dance,
Bound by desire's flame.

Latin Translation:
Calor intus surgit,
Cordibus in saltatione libidinosa colliduntur,
Flamma cupiditatis vinclis.

Reflection Prompt:
Think about how internal heat and external movements reflect your experiences of desire. How do physical and emotional sensations interplay in your passionate encounters?

Supplementary Content:
"Flamma cupiditatis vinclis" translates to "bound by desire's flame," emphasizing the binding and consuming nature of desire. The Latin version retains the imagery of rising heat and colliding hearts.

August 11th

Ecstasy

Haiku in English:
Sighs fill the still air,
In each touch, the world dissolves,
Pleasure's endless waves.

Latin Translation:
Suspiria aerem quietum implent,
In unoquoque tactu, mundus dissolvitur,
Undae interminatae voluptatis.

Reflection Prompt:

Consider how silence and touch create a sense of timelessness in intimate moments. How do such experiences make the world around you seem to disappear?

Supplementary Content:

"Suspiria aerem quietum implent" translates to "sighs fill the still air," setting a serene and intimate scene. The translation maintains the endless and immersive nature of pleasure described in the haiku.

August 12th

Ecstasy

Haiku in English:
Bodies intertwined,
Passion's symphony resounds,
In love's deepest core.

Latin Translation:
Corpora intorta,
Symphonia passionis resonat,
In ipso amore profundo.

Reflection Prompt:

Reflect on the metaphor of a symphony in relation to passion. How do multiple elements of intimacy come together to create a harmonious and profound experience for you?

Supplementary Content:

"Symphonia passionis resonat" captures the idea of passion's symphony resounding, emphasizing the musicality and depth of intimate experiences. The translation aims to convey the intertwined nature of bodies and the profound core of love.

August 13th

Intense connection

Haiku in English:
Bodies intertwine,
Passion's flame ignites the night,
Whispered sighs and heat.

Latin Translation:
Corpora nectuntur,
Flamma passionis noctem accendit,
Susurri et calor.

Reflection Prompt:

How do moments of physical intimacy reflect deeper emotional connections in your life? Reflect on a time when a shared moment with someone felt particularly significant.

Supplementary Content:

The Latin phrase "Flamma passionis noctem accendit" captures the vivid imagery of passion igniting the night, symbolizing intense emotional and physical connections. Translating this involved finding words that conveyed both the physical and emotional heat of the moment.

August 14th

Intense connection

Haiku in English:
Lust's fevered embrace,
Skin to skin, a primal dance,
Heartbeats wild and free.

Latin Translation:
Amplexus ardentis,
Cutis ad cutem, saltatio primitiva,
Pulsus ferox et liber.

Reflection Prompt:

What does a "primal dance" of connection mean to you? Consider how physical closeness can create a powerful, almost instinctual bond between people.

Supplementary Content:

"Saltatio primitiva" translates to "primal dance," emphasizing the raw, instinctive nature of physical desire. The challenge in translation was maintaining the intensity and freedom implied by "ferox et liber."

August 15th

Intense connection
Haiku in English:
Under moon's soft glow,
Lovers lost in ecstasy,
Time stands still for two.

Latin Translation:
Sub luna molli lumine,
Amantes in extasi amissi,
Tempus pro duobus stat.

Reflection Prompt:

Think about a time when you felt completely absorbed in a moment with someone special. How did it feel like time stood still?

Supplementary Content:

"Tempus pro duobus stat" emphasizes the timeless quality of intimate moments. The translation process focused on capturing the serene and almost magical ambiance created by the moonlight.

August 16th

Intense connection

Haiku in English:
Sheets twist and tangle,
Breathless whispers fill the air,
Night of burning need.

Latin Translation:
Lintea torquent et implicantur,
Susurri sine respiratu aerem implent,
Nox ardentis necessitatis.

Reflection Prompt:

Reflect on how physical and emotional needs intertwine. How does the presence of another person intensify these feelings?

Supplementary Content:

"Susurri sine respiratu" translates to "breathless whispers," conveying an atmosphere of intense need and intimacy. The Latin translation aims to evoke the sense of urgency and physical closeness.

August 17th

Intense connection

Haiku in English:
Fingers trace the line,
Where desire and love collide,
Soft as morning light.

Latin Translation:
Digiti lineam sequuntur,
Ubi cupiditas et amor colliduntur,
Molliter ut lumen matutinum.

Reflection Prompt:

How do you differentiate between desire and love in your relationships? Consider the moments where these feelings overlap.

Supplementary Content:

"Ubi cupiditas et amor colliduntur" captures the intersection of desire and love. The translation highlights the delicate balance between physical desire and emotional connection, much like the softness of morning light.

August 18th

Intense connection

Haiku in English:
Electric touch sparks,
A universe of pleasure,
In a single kiss.

Latin Translation:
Tactus electricus scintillat,
Universum voluptatis,
In uno osculo.

Reflection Prompt:

Think about a single touch or kiss that felt particularly powerful. What made it stand out and how did it connect you to the other person?

Supplementary Content:

"Universum voluptatis" conveys the idea of a vast universe contained within a moment of pleasure. The translation process involved finding a way to express the intensity and expansiveness of such moments.

August 19th

Intense connection

Haiku in English:
Passionate whispers,
Skin glows with desire's warmth,
Night of endless dreams.

Latin Translation:
Susurri ardentes,
Cutis splendet calore cupiditatis,
Nox somniorum sine fine.

Reflection Prompt:

Reflect on how whispers and quiet moments can communicate deep feelings. How do these intimate exchanges affect your relationships?

Supplementary Content:

"Cutis splendet calore cupiditatis" translates to "skin glows with desire's warmth," emphasizing the physical manifestation of desire. The translation aims to evoke the dreamy and endless nature of passionate nights.

August 20th

Intense connection

Haiku in English:
Breath mingles with sighs,
Hearts race in the shadowed night,
Love's fierce, wild embrace.

Latin Translation:
Spiritus cum susurris miscetur,
Cordibus in nocte umbrata properant,
Amplexus ferox et ferus amoris.

Reflection Prompt:

Consider how physical and emotional closeness can create a fierce, wild connection. How does the intensity of these moments impact you?

Supplementary Content:

"Amplexus ferox et ferus amoris" captures the wild and fierce embrace of love. The translation aims to convey the intensity and passion of such moments, blending physical and emotional elements.

August 21st

Intense connection

Haiku in English:
In the dark we dance,
Bodies speak in silent tongues,
Passion's secret song.

Latin Translation:
In tenebris saltamus,
Corpora tacitis linguis loquuntur,
Canticum secretum passionis.

Reflection Prompt:

Reflect on how non-verbal communication can express deep feelings. How do physical gestures and movements speak to you in moments of passion?

Supplementary Content:

"Corpora tacitis linguis loquuntur" translates to "bodies speak in silent tongues," emphasizing the power of non-verbal communication. The translation process focused on capturing the secrecy and intimacy of these interactions.

August 22nd

Intense connection

Haiku in English:
Flames of lust consume,
Every touch a new fire,
Burning through the night.

Latin Translation:
Flammae libidinis consumunt,
Omnis tactus novus ignis,
Per noctem ardens.

Reflection Prompt:

Consider how physical desire can feel all-consuming. How do these intense feelings shape your connections and interactions?

Supplementary Content:

"Flammae libidinis consumunt" translates to "flames of lust consume," emphasizing the intensity and all-encompassing nature of physical desire. The translation seeks to convey the sense of burning passion that lasts through the night.

August 23rd

Friendship

Haiku in English:
Life's fleeting moment,
Friends like stars in endless night,
Shine through darkest times.

Latin Translation:
Vita est momenta,
Amici ut astra nocte,
Lucent per tenebras.

Reflection Prompt:

How have your friends shined through the darkest times in your life? Reflect on a specific moment when a friend's support made a significant difference for you.

Supplementary Content:

The Latin translation, "Amici ut astra nocte," emphasizes the metaphor of friends as guiding stars. The use of "tenebras" (darkness) aligns with the idea that friends illuminate our lives during challenging times.

August 24th

Friendship

Haiku in English:
In the garden's peace,
Laughter of friends blooms brightly,
Seasons of the heart.

Latin Translation:
In horti pace,
Risus amicorum floret,
Temporibus cordis.

Reflection Prompt:

Consider the metaphor of a garden in relation to friendship. How does the laughter of friends bring peace and joy to your life?

Supplementary Content:

"Risus amicorum floret" translates to "the laughter of friends blooms," capturing the idea of friendship bringing life and color to our experiences, much like flowers in a garden.

August 25th

Friendship

Haiku in English:
Paths of life converge,
Bonds of friendship intertwine,
Stronger with each step.

Latin Translation:
Vitae viae conveniunt,
Vincula amicitiae nectuntur,
Fortiores cum passu.

Reflection Prompt:

Reflect on how your life's path has intertwined with those of your friends. How have your friendships grown stronger with each shared experience?

Supplementary Content:

"Vincula amicitiae nectuntur" emphasizes the intertwining of friendship bonds, suggesting a growing strength with each step taken together.

August 26th

Friendship

Haiku in English:
Whispering winds tell,
Stories of friends' shared journeys,
Eternal echoes.

Latin Translation:
Venti susurrantes narrant,
Fabulas itinerum communium,
Echoes aeterni.

Reflection Prompt:

Think about the stories shared with friends over the years. How do these memories continue to resonate and impact your life?

Supplementary Content:

"Fabulas itinerum communium" translates to "stories of shared journeys," highlighting the lasting impact of shared experiences with friends, like whispers carried by the wind.

August 27th

Friendship

Haiku in English:
Autumn leaves will fall,
Friends remain through winter's chill,
Warmth in every word.

Latin Translation:
Folia cadunt autumnales,
Amici manent hieme frigus,
Calor in omni verbo.

Reflection Prompt:

Consider the imagery of seasons in relation to friendship. How have your friends provided warmth and support during the "winter" periods of your life?

Supplementary Content:

"Amici manent hieme frigus" emphasizes the steadfastness of friends during difficult times, using the metaphor of winter's chill to represent challenges and the warmth of words to signify support.

August 28th

Friendship

Haiku in English:
Moonlight on the lake,
Reflections of friendship's light,
Gentle, ever near.

Latin Translation:
Lumen lunae in lacu,
Reflectiones lucis amicitiae,
Leniter, semper prope.

Reflection Prompt:

Think about a serene moment shared with a friend. How do these gentle and peaceful times reflect the light and presence of your friendship?

Supplementary Content:

"Reflectiones lucis amicitiae" translates to "reflections of friendship's light," capturing the gentle and continuous presence of friendship, much like the steady glow of moonlight on water.

August 29th

Friendship

Haiku in English:
Morning dew on grass,
Friends' presence, soft and soothing,
Fresh start every day.

Latin Translation:
Ros mane in herba,
Praesentia amicorum mollis,
Initium recens cotidie.

Reflection Prompt:

Consider how the presence of friends provides a fresh start and a sense of renewal. How do your friends help you face each new day with positivity?

Supplementary Content:

"Praesentia amicorum mollis" emphasizes the soft and soothing presence of friends, likened to the refreshing quality of morning dew, symbolizing new beginnings.

August 30th

Friendship

Haiku in English:
Silent snowy night,
Friends' warmth inside the cabin,
Hearts glow by the fire.

Latin Translation:
Noctis silentium nivis,
Calor amicorum in casula,
Cordibus coruscent ad ignem.

Reflection Prompt:

Think about a cozy, quiet moment shared with friends. How does their warmth and companionship create a sense of comfort and belonging?

Supplementary Content:

"Calor amicorum in casula" translates to "the warmth of friends in the cabin," evoking the image of a safe and warm haven provided by friendship during cold and silent times.

August 31st

Friendship

Haiku in English:
River's gentle flow,
Friends beside on life's long path,
Together we stand.

Latin Translation:
Fluvius lenis fluxus,
Amici iuxta in via longa vitae,
Una stamus.

Reflection Prompt:

Reflect on the continuous support of friends as you journey through life. How do they help you stay strong and steady, much like the gentle flow of a river?

Supplementary Content:

"Amici iuxta in via longa vitae" emphasizes the steady and supportive presence of friends, drawing a parallel to the gentle and constant flow of a river, symbolizing life's journey.

September 1st

Friendship

Haiku in English:
Blossoms in the spring,
Friendship grows with every bloom,
Seasons never end.

Latin Translation:
Flores in vere,
Amicitia crescit cum omni flore,
Tempora numquam desinunt.

Reflection Prompt:

Consider the growth of friendships over time, much like flowers blooming in spring. How have your friendships evolved and flourished through different seasons of life?

Supplementary Content:

"Amicitia crescit cum omni flore" translates to "friendship grows with every bloom," emphasizing the continuous and ever-renewing nature of friendships, akin to the perpetual cycles of the seasons.

September 2nd

Opinion

Haiku in English:
Silence fills the air,
Opinions lost in the void,
Safe but empty minds.

Latin Translation:
Silentium aerem implet,
Opiniones in vacuo amissae,
Mentes tutas sed inanes.

Reflection Prompt:

How does the absence of differing opinions affect personal growth and societal progress? Reflect on a time when you avoided sharing your opinion.

Supplementary Content:

This haiku explores the idea of a society where voices are silenced for the sake of safety. In Latin, "vacuo" emphasizes the emptiness created by this silence, highlighting a key difference in nuance from the English version.

September 3rd

Opinion

Haiku in English:
Risk is shunned today,
Voices whisper in the dark,
Safety stifles thought.

Latin Translation:
Periculum hodie evitatur,
Voces in tenebris susurrant,
Securitas cogitationem suffocat.

Reflection Prompt:

Consider the balance between safety and freedom of expression. When does the desire for safety begin to stifle creativity and critical thinking?

Supplementary Content:

The Latin word "suffocat" (stifles) vividly captures the suffocating effect of excessive safety on thought, a concept crucial to understanding the poem's message.

September 4th

Opinion

Haiku in English:
Unseen dangers lurk,
Behind screens and guarded hearts,
Fearful of new views.

Latin Translation:
Latent pericula invisa,
Post screens et corda custodita,
Novorum opinionum metuentes.

Reflection Prompt:

How do modern technologies contribute to a culture of fear and isolation? Reflect on your own experience with social media.

Supplementary Content:

"Metuentes" (fearing) in Latin intensifies the emotion conveyed, emphasizing the anxiety surrounding new opinions and perspectives in contemporary society. It corresponds to the Greek term "σεβόμενοι τ ν Θεόν" (English: "respecting God")

September 5th

Opinion

Haiku in English:
No risk, no surprise,
A world wrapped in bubble wrap,
Dull yet free from harm.

Latin Translation:
Nullum periculum, nulla admiratio,
Mundus in involucro bullarum involutus,
Insulsus tamen a damno liber.

Reflection Prompt:

What are the consequences of eliminating all risks from our lives? Discuss the potential downsides of a completely risk-free world.

Supplementary Content:

The metaphor of "involucro bullarum" (bubble wrap) in Latin provides a striking visual of overprotection, linking it to the loss of excitement and growth.

September 6th

Opinion

Haiku in English:
Echoes in the halls,
Same thoughts over and again,
Diverse voices fade.

Latin Translation:
Resonant in atriis,
Eadem cogitationes iterum atque iterum,
Vocibus diversis evanescunt.

Reflection Prompt:

Why is it important to have diverse voices and opinions in any community? Reflect on a situation where a lack of diversity in thought was detrimental.

Supplementary Content:

"Evanescunt" (fade) in Latin underscores the gradual disappearance of diversity, a slow but significant loss that affects the vibrancy of a community.

September 7th

Opinion

Haiku in English:
Opinions withheld,
Fearing sharp tongues and cold eyes,
Safe but isolated.

Latin Translation:
Opiniones retentae,
Metuentes acuta linguas et frigida oculis,
Securus sed solitarius.

Reflection Prompt:

What are the psychological effects of withholding opinions? Share an experience where you felt isolated due to fear of judgment.

Supplementary Content:

The juxtaposition of "acuta" (sharp) and "frigida" (cold) in Latin highlights the dual nature of social judgments, reinforcing the theme of isolation despite safety.

September 8th

Opinion

Haiku in English:
Unpredictable,
Life's rich tapestry now bland,
Riskless, dull routine.

Latin Translation:
Imprevidibilis,
Vitae tapetia nunc insulsa,
Sine periculo, taediosa consuetudo.

Reflection Prompt:

How does predictability affect your daily life? Discuss the importance
of unpredictability in maintaining a vibrant and fulfilling existence.

Supplementary Content:

The word "imprevidibilis" (unpredictable) serves as a stark contrast
to "taediosa consuetudo" (dull routine), emphasizing the cost of
eliminating risks.

September 9th

Opinion

Haiku in English:
Guarded hearts we keep,
Sheltered from the world's harsh winds,
Yet we long for more.

Latin Translation
Corda custodita servamus,
A ventis asperis mundi tecta,
Tamen plura desideramus.

Reflection Prompt:

Reflect on the balance between protecting oneself and experiencing life fully. How can one maintain this balance effectively?

Supplementary Content:

"Desideramus" (long for) in Latin conveys a deep yearning, capturing the human desire for a richer, more engaging life despite the need for protection.

September 10th

Opinion

Haiku in English:
Freedom is a dream,
Chained by fear of offense,
We stay silent, still.

Latin Translation
Libertas somnium est,
Catenae timore offensionis,
Tacemus, immoti.

Reflection Prompt:

What does freedom of speech mean to you? Reflect on the impact of self-censorship on personal and societal levels.

Supplementary Content:

"Catenae" (chains) vividly illustrate the constraints imposed by fear, underscoring the contrast between the ideal of freedom and the reality of silence.

September 11th

Opinion

Haiku in English:
Critique is a threat,
Conformity is our shield,
Comfort over truth.

Latin Translation
Critica est minatio,
Conformitas est scutum nostrum,
Consolatio supra veritatem.

Reflection Prompt:

Discuss the role of critique in personal growth. How does conformity inhibit progress?

Supplementary Content:

"Scutum" (shield) in Latin signifies protection, yet it also implies limitation, highlighting the conflict between comfort and the pursuit of truth.

September 12th

Opinion

Haiku in English:
Whispers in the dark,
Opinions feared and hidden,
Light cannot reach them.

Latin Translation
Susurri in tenebris,
Opiniones timidae et celatae,
Lux ad eos non pervenit.

Reflection Prompt:

Why is transparency important in discussions and debates? Reflect on the consequences of hidden opinions.

Supplementary Content:

The phrase "lux ad eos non pervenit" (light cannot reach them) in Latin emphasizes the idea that hidden opinions prevent enlightenment and growth.

September 13th

Opinion

Haiku in English:
Sheltered from the storm,
But missing the rain's sweet touch,
Safe but unfulfilled.

Latin Translation
Ab tempestatibus protectus,
Sed carentes dulci tactu pluviae,
Tutus sed inplectus.

Reflection Prompt:

Reflect on the idea of being overly sheltered. How can too much protection lead to a sense of unfulfillment?

Supplementary Content:

"Carentes dulci tactu pluviae" (missing the rain's sweet touch) in Latin captures the paradox of being protected yet yearning for enriching experiences.

September 14th

Opinion

Haiku in English:
Careful what we say,
Words are weighed and filtered clean,
Truth diluted, lost.

Latin Translation
Attenti quid dicimus,
Verba pensantur et purgantur,
Veritas diluta, perdita.

Reflection Prompt:

How does excessive filtering of words affect communication? Discuss the importance of honesty in dialogue.

Supplementary Content:

"Veritas diluta, perdita" (truth diluted, lost) in Latin succinctly conveys the erosion of truth through over-caution, highlighting a key theme of the poem.

September 15th

Opinion

Haiku in English:
Living in a shell,
Protected from life's chaos,
But missing its song.

Latin Translation
In testudine vivimus,
A vitae tumultu protecti,
Sed carentes eius cantu.

Reflection Prompt:

Consider the trade-offs between safety and experience. How can one embrace the chaos of life while maintaining a sense of security?

Supplementary Content:

"Eius cantu" (its song) in Latin metaphorically represents the richness of life's experiences, contrasting with the protection provided by the "testudine" (shell).

September 16th

Opinion

Haiku in English:
Hiding from the storm,
Opinions locked away tight,
Safety over growth.

Latin Translation
A tempestate latentes,
Opiniones arcte clausae,
Securitas supra incrementum.

Reflection Prompt:

Reflect on the impact of prioritizing safety over personal and intellectual growth. How can one achieve a balance between the two?

Supplementary Content:

"Arcte clausae" (locked away tight) in Latin emphasizes the restrictive nature of hiding opinions, underscoring the theme of stagnation versus growth.

September 17th

Regressiveness

Regressiveness

Haiku in English:
Cotton candy dreams,
Nostalgia wraps us in pink,
Sweet but void of truth.

Latin Translation
Somnia saccharina,
Nostalgia nos in rosa involvit,
Dulcis sed veritate vacua.

Reflection Prompt:

What are some "cotton candy dreams" in your life? How do they make you feel both comforted and unfulfilled?

Supplementary Content:

The translation process for this haiku involved finding the delicate balance between the dreamlike quality of nostalgia and its underlying emptiness. "Somnia saccharina" captures the sweetness and superficiality of these dreams.

September 18th

Regressiveness

Haiku in English:
Fleeting memories,
Soft and sweet as summer's breeze,
Illusions we crave.

Latin Translation
Memoriae fugaces,
Mollia et dulcia ut aestatis aura,
Illusiones desideramus.

Reflection Prompt:

Think of a fleeting memory that brings you joy. Why do you think you crave such illusions?

Supplementary Content:

Translating "summer's breeze" to "aestatis aura" conveys the ephemeral and gentle nature of these memories, emphasizing their transient beauty.

September 19th

Regressiveness

Haiku in English:
In the past we drown,
Wrapped in sweet, sticky comfort,
Future fades away.

Latin Translation
In praeterito mergimur,
In dulci, adhaerente consolatione involuti,
Futurum evanescit.

Reflection Prompt:

How does dwelling on the past affect your perception of the future?

Supplementary Content:

The Latin word "adhaerente" (sticky) effectively portrays the clingy nature of comforting memories, while "futurum evanescit" (future fades) highlights the overshadowing effect of nostalgia.

September 20th

Regressiveness

Haiku in English:
Cotton candy clouds,
Shielding us from harsh sunlight,
Comfort in the fluff.

Latin Translation
Nubes saccharinae,
Nos a solis luce aspera protegentes,
Consolatio in mollicie.

Reflection Prompt:

What are your "cotton candy clouds" that protect you from reality? How do they comfort you?

Supplementary Content:

"Nubes saccharinae" (cotton candy clouds) illustrates how comforting illusions can act as shields, offering temporary solace from life's harsh truths.

September 21st

Regressiveness

Haiku in English:
Nostalgia's embrace,
Holds us in a pink cocoon,
Safe but unfulfilled.

Latin Translation
Amplexus nostalgiae,
Nos in rosa cocco tenet,
Tutum sed inplectum.

Reflection Prompt:

Reflect on a time when nostalgia made you feel safe. Did it also leave you feeling unfulfilled?

Supplementary Content:

"Rosa cocco" (pink cocoon) effectively captures the idea of being wrapped in nostalgia, where "tutum sed inplectum" (safe but unfulfilled) emphasizes the bittersweet nature of such an embrace.

September 22nd

Regressiveness

Haiku in English:
Sugary past calls,
Soft whispers of yesteryears,
False sweetness we chase.

Latin Translation
Saccharina praeterita vocant,
Mollia susurrans annorum praeteritorum,
Falsam dulcedinem persequimur.

Reflection Prompt:

Why do you think we often chase after the false sweetness of the past?

Supplementary Content:

The phrase "falsam dulcedinem" (false sweetness) in Latin poignantly illustrates the deceptive allure of nostalgic memories.

September 23rd

Regressiveness

Haiku in English:
Dreams of candy floss,
Draw us back to simpler times,
Harmless yet so thin.

Latin Translation
Somnia de flossa saccharo,
Nos ad tempora simpliciora retrahunt,
Innocua sed tam tenui.

Reflection Prompt:

What "simpler times" do you find yourself drawn to, and why might
they seem harmless but insubstantial?

Supplementary Content:

"Flossa saccharo" (candy floss) is a vivid metaphor for the fragile and
superficial nature of these nostalgic dreams.

September 24th

Regressiveness

Haiku in English:
Pink clouds in the sky,
Drifting through our wistful minds,
Ephemeral joy.

Latin Translation
Nubes rosae in caelo,
Per mentes desiderantes fluitantes,
Gaudium ephemerum.

Reflection Prompt:

Can you recall a moment of ephemeral joy from your past? How did it drift through your mind?

Supplementary Content:

"Gaudium ephemerum" (ephemeral joy) captures the fleeting nature of happiness that nostalgia often brings, emphasizing its temporary quality.

September 25th

Regressiveness
Haiku in English:
Clinging to the past,
Sugar-coating memories,
Reality fades.

Latin Translation
Praeterito adhaerentes,
Memoriae saccharo coopertae,
Realitas evanescit.

Reflection Prompt:

How do you sugar-coat your memories, and how does this affect your grasp on reality?

Supplementary Content:

"Saccharo coopertae" (sugar-coated) highlights how nostalgia can alter our perception of past events, making them sweeter than they were.

September 26th

Regressiveness

Haiku in English:
Wrapped in candy hues,
Soft nostalgia blinds our sight,
Truth hidden beneath.

Latin Translation
In saccharinis coloribus involuti,
Mollis nostalgia visum nostrum caecat,
Veritas subter abscondita.

Reflection Prompt:

How does nostalgia blind you to the truth? What truths might be hidden beneath your nostalgic memories?

Supplementary Content:

The imagery of being "involuti" (wrapped) in "saccharinis coloribus" (candy hues) illustrates how these comforting illusions can obscure reality.

September 27th

Regressiveness

Haiku in English:
Nostalgia's sweet trap,
Candy-coated lullabies,
Empty melodies.

Latin Translation:
Captus dulcis nostalgiae,
Cantica saccharo cooperta,
Vacua melodias.

Reflection Prompt:

Can you identify a "sweet trap" of nostalgia in your life? What makes its melody feel empty?

Supplementary Content:

"Captus dulcis" (sweet trap) and "vacua melodias" (empty melodies) emphasize the enticing yet hollow nature of nostalgic comfort.

September 28th

Regressiveness

Haiku in English:
Craving soft comforts,
In a haze of pink delight,
Lost in past's embrace.

Latin Translation:
Mollia desiderantes solacia,
In nube rosae deliciae,
In amplexu praeteriti amissi.

Reflection Prompt:

What soft comforts do you crave, and how does this affect your connection to the present?

Supplementary Content:

"Nube rosae deliciae" (haze of pink delight) effectively conveys the dreamlike state induced by nostalgic memories.

September 29th

Regressiveness

Haiku in English:
Pink hues of the past,
Wrap us in their gentle glow,
Substance fades away.

Latin Translation:
Colora rosa praeteriti,
Nos in molli lumine involvunt,
Substantia evanescit.

Reflection Prompt:

How do the "pink hues" of your past make you feel? Why might their substance fade away?

Supplementary Content:

"Substantia evanescit" (substance fades away) underscores the fleeting and often unsubstantial nature of nostalgic memories.

September 30th

Regressiveness

Haiku in English:
Sweetness coats our minds,
Nostalgia's gentle fingers,
Hide the bitter truth.

Latin Translation:
Dulcedo mentes nostras operit,
Mollia digita nostalgiae,
Veritatem amarum celant.

Reflection Prompt:

What bitter truths might be hidden beneath the sweetness of your nostalgia?

Supplementary Content:

"Veritatem amarum celant" (hide the bitter truth) conveys the idea that nostalgia can obscure harsh realities.

October 1st

Regressiveness

Haiku in English:
In cotton candy,
We find fleeting happiness,
But no lasting peace.

Latin Translation:
In saccharina,
Fugacem felicitatem invenimus,
Sed nullam pacem durabilem.

Reflection Prompt:

Reflect on a time when you found fleeting happiness in something insubstantial. Did it bring you lasting peace?

Supplementary Content:

"Nullam pacem durabilem" (no lasting peace) highlights the temporary and ultimately unsatisfying nature of such happiness.

October 2nd

Vanity

Haiku in English:
Vanity thrives strong,
Sellers exploit desires,
Market's empty song.

Latin Translation:
Vanitas viget,
Venditores cupiditates explent,
Carmen vacuum mercatus.

Reflection Prompt:

How does modern advertising exploit our desires for things we don't need? Have you ever bought something due to clever marketing rather than necessity?

Supplementary Content:

Translating "vanity" to "vanitas" captures the historical depth of the term. In Latin literature, "vanitas" often reflected not just vanity but also futility and emptiness, enhancing the poem's meaning.

October 3rd

Vanity

Haiku in English:
False smiles and fake charm,
Sleazy sellers bait the vain,
Market's shallow heart.

Latin Translation:
Falsa risus et decus,
Venditores viles vanos alliciunt,
Cordis levitas mercatus.

Reflection Prompt:

Consider a time when you felt pressured to buy something. Was it the product itself or the salesperson's tactics that influenced your decision?

Supplementary Content:

The Latin "falsa risus" and "decus" emphasize the deceptive nature of the smiles and charm, highlighting the duplicity in commercial interactions.

October 4th

Vanity

Haiku in English:
Shiny trinkets sold,
Vain hearts buy what they don't need,
Market fattened well.

Latin Translation:
Splendentia ornamenta vendita,
Cordia vana quid non egent emunt,
Mercatus bene pinguis.

Reflection Prompt:

Why are we attracted to shiny and flashy objects? How does this reflect on our values and priorities?

Supplementary Content:

The phrase "splendentia ornamenta" underscores the allure of superficial beauty in consumer culture, aligning with the haiku's critique of materialism.

October 5th

Vanity

Haiku in English:
Vain eyes see glitter,
Sleazy words seal the deal fast,
Market swells with pride.

Latin Translation:
Oculi vani splendorem vident,
Verba vilium celeriter pacta firmant,
Mercatus superbia intumescit.

Reflection Prompt:

Reflect on a purchase you made based purely on appearance. Did it meet your expectations or disappoint you?

Supplementary Content:

"Superbia" in Latin not only means pride but can also imply arrogance, enriching the haiku's message about the market's inflated self-importance.

October 6th

Vanity

Haiku in English:
Useless goods abound,
Sellers prey on vanity,
Market's empty gold.

Latin Translation:
Merces inutiles abundant,
Venditores vanitatem praedantur,
Aurum vacuum mercatus.

Reflection Prompt:

What are some examples of "useless goods" in today's market? Why do we continue to buy them?

Supplementary Content:

The term "aurum vacuum" (empty gold) in Latin draws a parallel with the English idiom "fool's gold," emphasizing the worthlessness of the goods despite their appealing appearance.

October 7th

Vanity

Haiku in English:
Mirror's empty praise,
Sleazy sellers know the game,
Market thrives on lies.

Latin Translation:
Speculi laudatio vacua,
Venditores viles ludum norunt,
Mercatus mendaciis viget.

Reflection Prompt:

How does society's obsession with image and appearance fuel consumer behavior?

Supplementary Content:

"Speculi laudatio vacua" metaphorically represents the superficial validation we seek from others, highlighting the hollow nature of such praise.

October 8th

Vanity

Haiku in English:
Vanity's delight,
Sellers craft their perfect pitch,
Market's hollow gain.

Latin Translation:
Vanitatis gaudium,
Venditores perfectam orationem fabricant,
Mercatus lucrum inanem.

Reflection Prompt:

Think about an advertisement that left a strong impression on you.
What techniques did it use to appeal to your desires?

Supplementary Content:

"Perfectam orationem" in Latin suggests a meticulously crafted
speech, underscoring the calculated nature of marketing strategies.

October 9th

Vanity

Haiku in English:
Sleazy salesman's grin,
Vain buyers fall for the show,
Market's endless spin.

Latin Translation:
Risus vilis venditoris,
Emptores vani spectaculo capiuntur,
Mercatus rotatio infinita.

Reflection Prompt:

How do sales tactics manipulate our emotions? Are there ways to become more aware of these manipulations?

Supplementary Content:

"Rotatio infinita" conveys the perpetual cycle of consumerism, capturing the relentless nature of the market.

October 10th

Vanity

Haiku in English:
Glimmer in the eye,
Sellers know what fools will buy,
Market's empty cry.

Latin Translation:
Splendor in oculo,
Venditores sciunt quid stulti emant,
Clamor vacuus mercatus.

Reflection Prompt:

What role does social media play in perpetuating consumerism and vanity?

Supplementary Content:

The translation "clamor vacuus" evokes an empty outcry, suggesting that the market's allure is ultimately hollow and unfulfilling.

October 11th

Vanity

Haiku in English:
Vain hearts never filled,
Sellers feast on empty needs,
Market's bloated build.

Latin Translation:
Cordia vana numquam plena,
Venditores inanibus necessitatibus
vescuntur,
Aedificium inflatum mercatus.

Reflection Prompt:

Why do we continue to seek satisfaction in material possessions despite knowing they won't bring lasting happiness?

Supplementary Content:

"Aedificium inflatum" likens the market to a bloated structure, ready to collapse under its own weight, symbolizing unsustainable consumer practices.

October 12th

Vanity

Haiku in English:
Empty promises,
Sleazy sellers charm the vain,
Market's hollow bliss.

Latin Translation:
Promissa vacua,
Venditores viles vanos fascinant,
Beata vacuitas mercatus.

Reflection Prompt:

How do empty promises in advertising affect our trust in brands and products?

Supplementary Content:

"Beata vacuitas" juxtaposes the concepts of happiness and emptiness, highlighting the false sense of joy consumerism promises.

October 13th

Vanity

Haiku in English:
Vanity buys lies,
Sleazy sales make pockets fat,
Market's fleeting highs.

Latin Translation:
Vanitas mendacia emit,
Venditiones viles crassos loculos faciunt,
Mercatus transitoria summa.

Reflection Prompt:

Consider a time you regretted a purchase. What led to that decision, and how did you feel afterward?

Supplementary Content:

"Transitoria summa" captures the temporary nature of consumer satisfaction, emphasizing that the highs are brief and unsustainable.

October 14th

Vanity

Haiku in English:
Vain dreams sold as gold,
Sleazy sellers find their marks,
Market's tale retold.

Latin Translation:
Somnia vana ut aurum vendita,
Venditores viles suas metas inveniunt,
Fabula mercatus redit.

Reflection Prompt:

How does consumerism shape our dreams and aspirations? Are they truly our own?

Supplementary Content:

"Fabula mercatus" implies a recurring story, suggesting that the cycle of vanity and consumerism is an age-old tale, continuously retold.

October 15th

Vanity

Haiku in English:
Vain desires grow,
Sellers spin their webs so sly,
Market's endless show.

Latin Translation:
Desideria vana crescunt,
Venditores suas telas callide nectunt,
Spectaculum infinitum mercatus.

Reflection Prompt:

What are some ways to resist the allure of consumer culture? Can we find fulfillment elsewhere?

Supplementary Content:

"Spectaculum infinitum" reflects the never-ending performance of the market, portraying consumerism as an endless spectacle designed to captivate and deceive.

October 16th

Vanity

Haiku in English:
Sleazy words entice,
Vain hearts fall for worthless wares,
Market's hollow vice.

Latin Translation:
Verba viles alliciunt,
Cordia vana merces nullius pretii capiunt,
Vitium vacuum mercatus.

Reflection Prompt:

How can we differentiate between genuine needs and those created by manipulative marketing?

Supplementary Content:

"Vitium vacuum" combines the ideas of vice and emptiness, underscoring the moral and existential void that consumerism can create.

October 17th

Cruelty

Haiku in English:
Mean words, hearts wounded,
Laughter hides cruel intent,
Kindness is silent.

Latin Translation:
Verba crudelia,
Corda vulnera latent,
Tacita benignitas.

Reflection Prompt:

Have you ever experienced someone using humor to mask their cruelty? How did it make you feel, and how did you respond?

Supplementary Content:

This haiku highlights the pain inflicted by seemingly playful banter that is, in reality, hurtful. The contrast between laughter and silence underscores the often unseen impact of mean words.

October 18th

Cruelty

Haiku in English:
Fools on their high thrones,
Criticizing, shouting loud,
Wisdom stands alone.

Latin Translation:
Stulti in thronis,
Criticantes, clamantes,
Sapientia sola.

Reflection Prompt:

Think about a time when someone loudly criticized others. How did the quiet wisdom of others around them contrast with their behavior?

Supplementary Content:

This poem illustrates the isolating nature of true wisdom amidst loud, critical voices. It invites reflection on the power of quiet strength.

October 19th

Cruelty

Haiku in English:
Pedestals they seek,
Dragging others to the ground,
True worth stays unseen.

Latin Translation:
Pedestallos quaerunt,
Alios ad terram trahunt,
Vera virtus latet.

Reflection Prompt:

Why do some people feel the need to put others down to elevate themselves? How can you recognize true worth in yourself and others?

Supplementary Content:

The imagery of pedestals and dragging others down symbolizes the destructive behavior of those who seek to elevate themselves at others' expense.

October 20th

Cruelty

Haiku in English:
Silent grace remains,
Rascal voices pierce the air,
Gentle souls withdraw.

Latin Translation:
Gratia manet,
Vocibus sceleri aequat,
Animis mollibus.

Reflection Prompt:

Have you ever chosen to withdraw from a situation rather than engage with negative voices? How did this decision affect you?

Supplementary Content:

This haiku captures the retreat of gentle souls in the face of loud, disruptive individuals, highlighting the strength found in silence and grace.

October 21st

Cruelty

Haiku in English:
Mockery their game,
Entertaining at your cost,
True joy found in peace.

Latin Translation:
Iocus risus,
Expendis, pretio tuo,
Vera gaudia pax.

Reflection Prompt:

Can you recall a situation where mockery was used as entertainment? How did it contrast with moments of true joy you have experienced?

Supplementary Content:

The poem contrasts mockery with genuine joy, suggesting that true happiness is found in peace rather than in the suffering of others.

October 22nd

Cruelty

Haiku in English:
Voices rise in scorn,
Cruelty masked as humor,
Kind hearts turn away.

Latin Translation:
Voces contumeliae,
Crudelitas larvata,
Mansueta corda.

Reflection Prompt:

Why do kind hearts often turn away from scorn and cruelty? How can you foster an environment where kindness prevails?

Supplementary Content:

This haiku emphasizes the tendency of kind individuals to distance themselves from cruelty, reflecting on the importance of a nurturing environment.

October 23rd

Cruelty

Haiku in English:
In shadows they stand,
Casting stones with bitter glee,
Love's light can't be dimmed.

Latin Translation:
In umbris stant,
Saxa ieciunt laeti,
Amoris lux clara.

Reflection Prompt:

How can you maintain a loving and positive outlook even when faced with negativity?

Supplementary Content:

The imagery of shadows and stones represents the hidden and harmful actions of others, contrasted with the enduring light of love.

October 24th

Cruelty

Haiku in English:
Harsh words ripple out,
Echoes of unkind jesting,
Respect lost, tears flow.

Latin Translation:
Verba acerba volant,
Resonant, ioco crudo,
Respectus lacrimae.

Reflection Prompt:

Think about a time when harsh words affected you or someone you know. How can you ensure your words build others up instead?

Supplementary Content:

This poem explores the lasting impact of harsh words and unkind jokes, emphasizing the loss of respect and the emotional damage caused.

October 25th

Cruelty

Haiku in English:
Pedestals of sand,
Erode with each cruel remark,
True strength lifts others.

Latin Translation:
Pedestalli arenae,
Crudelibus verbis,
Vera vires alunt.

Reflection Prompt:

Why are pedestals built on cruelty ultimately unsustainable? How can true strength be demonstrated?

Supplementary Content:

The metaphor of sand pedestals suggests the instability of a foundation built on cruelty, while true strength is shown through uplifting others.

October 26th

Cruelty

Haiku in English:
Dating, shouting loud,
Impossible connections,
Quiet love prevails.

Latin Translation:
Dulce, clamans,
Connexiones non fiunt,
Tranquillus amor.

Reflection Prompt:

How do loud and superficial interactions hinder genuine connections? What role does quiet, sincere communication play in relationships?

Supplementary Content:

This haiku critiques the loud and superficial nature of some social interactions, advocating for the quiet and genuine connections that form true relationships.

October 27th

Cruelty

Haiku in English:
Mean words, laughter shared,
At another's expense, cruel,
Kindness whispers soft.

Latin Translation:
Verba crudelia,
Risus participatus,
Benignitas sussurrat.

Reflection Prompt:

How can you respond with kindness in situations where mean words are shared for entertainment?

Supplementary Content:

This poem contrasts the loud cruelty of shared mean words with the quiet, persistent whisper of kindness, encouraging a gentle response to negativity.

October 28th

Cruelty

Haiku in English:
Entertain with grace,
Lifting hearts with gentle praise,
Mockery fades fast.

Latin Translation:
Gratia hilaris,
Cordium levamen,
Derisio cito.

Reflection Prompt:

Reflect on a time when gentle praise uplifted you or someone else. How does this compare to moments of mockery?

Supplementary Content:

The haiku promotes the idea that graceful entertainment through gentle praise is more lasting and meaningful than mockery, which fades quickly.

October 29th

Cruelty

Haiku in English:
Educated fools,
Devoid of empathy's touch,
Fall from their high perch.

Latin Translation:
Docti stulti,
Carent tactu pietatis,
Altis cadunt.

Reflection Prompt:

What does it mean to be educated yet lack empathy? How can empathy enhance true wisdom?

Supplementary Content:

This poem critiques those who possess knowledge but lack empathy, suggesting that true wisdom includes understanding and compassion.

October 30th

Cruelty

Haiku in English:
Rascals, unlearned,
Build their thrones on others' pain,
Wisdom walks away.

Latin Translation:
Rogues indocti,
Aedificant thronos,
Sapientia discedit.

Reflection Prompt:

Why is it unwise to build success on the suffering of others? How can you ensure your achievements uplift rather than harm?

Supplementary Content:

This haiku highlights the futility and destructiveness of building success on others' pain, contrasting it with the wise choice of walking away.

October 31th

Cruelty

Haiku in English:
Peaceful hearts endure,
Cruel tongues wither in silence,
Love blooms quietly.

Latin Translation:
Cordia pacata,
Crudelia labra,
Amor quiete floret.

Reflection Prompt:

How can maintaining a peaceful heart help you endure cruelty? In what ways does love quietly bloom in your life?

Supplementary Content:

This haiku celebrates the endurance of peaceful hearts and the quiet blossoming of love, suggesting that cruelty ultimately fades in the face of persistent kindness.

November 1st

Useless stuff

Haiku in English:
Pushers of trinkets,
Carbon footprints long ignored,
Support still persists.

Latin Translation:
Venditores rerum inutilium,
Vestigia carbonis neglecta,
Auxilium tamen manet.

Reflection Prompt:

How does the persistence of support for wasteful products affect our environment?

Supplementary Content:

This haiku and its translation emphasize the environmental cost of producing and selling unnecessary items. The phrase "vestigia carbonis" (carbon footprints) highlights the long-term impact on our planet.

November 2nd

Useless stuff

Haiku in English:
Useless things abound,
Entrepreneurs keep pushing,
Planet pays the price.

Latin Translation:
Res inutiles abundant,
Entreprendedores promovent,
Terra pretium solvit.

Reflection Prompt:

What are some steps individuals can take to reduce their carbon footprint?

Supplementary Content:

"Terra pretium solvit" (the planet pays the price) underscores the environmental burden of excessive consumerism, emphasizing the need for more sustainable practices.

November 3rd

Useless stuff

Haiku in English:
Carbon talks long past,
Yet support for waste persists,
Change is slow to come.

Latin Translation:
Conloquia carbonis vetera,
Sed auxilium prodigi manet,
Mutatio tarda venit.

Reflection Prompt:

Why do you think change in environmental policies is often slow?

Supplementary Content:

This haiku reflects on the slow progress in environmental change, despite longstanding discussions on carbon footprints. The translation captures this delay with "mutatio tarda venit" (change is slow to come).

November 4th

Useless stuff

Haiku in English:
Corona has shown,
Life without endless trinkets,
Is more than just fine.

Latin Translation:
Corona monstravit,
Vita sine trinkets infinitis,
Est plus quam satis.

Reflection Prompt:

How did your perspective on material possessions change during the pandemic?

Supplementary Content:

"Corona monstravit" (Corona has shown) points to the lessons learned during the pandemic about living with less, suggesting a shift towards valuing essentials over excess.

November 5th

Useless stuff

Haiku in English:
Trinkets lose their charm,
In crisis, needs become clear,
Essentials now reign.

Latin Translation:
Trinkets gratiam amittunt,
In crisi, necessitates evident,
Essentialia nunc regnant.

Reflection Prompt:

What essentials became more important to you during a crisis, and why?

Supplementary Content:

"Essentialia nunc regnant" (essentials now reign) highlights the shift in priorities during challenging times, emphasizing the importance of distinguishing between needs and wants.

November 6th

Useless stuff

Haiku in English:
Entrepreneurs sell,
Useless items far and wide,
Carbon trail expands.

Latin Translation:
Entreprendedores vendunt,
Res inutiles longe lateque,
Vestigia carbonis dilatantur.

Reflection Prompt:

What can entrepreneurs do to minimize the environmental impact of their businesses?

Supplementary Content:

"Vestigia carbonis dilatantur" (carbon trail expands) illustrates the growing environmental impact of widespread consumerism, urging for more responsible business practices.

November 7th

Useless stuff

Haiku in English:
Support for the waste,
Despite the carbon outcry,
Habit hard to break.

Latin Translation:
Auxilium pro prodigo,
Praeter clamorem carbonis,
Consuetudo dura frangere.

Reflection Prompt:

What habits do you find hardest to change in your efforts to live sustainably?

Supplementary Content:

"Consuetudo dura frangere" (habit hard to break) captures the challenge of changing deeply ingrained habits, even when there is a clear environmental need.

November 8th

Useless stuff
Haiku in English:
Living without waste,
Corona taught us this truth,
Less can be much more.

Latin Translation:
Vivere sine prodigo,
Corona hanc veritatem docuit,
Minus potest esse plus.

Reflection Prompt:

In what ways did you simplify your life during the pandemic, and what were the outcomes?

Supplementary Content:

"Minus potest esse plus" (less can be much more) conveys the idea that reducing waste can lead to greater fulfillment, a lesson reinforced by the pandemic.

November 9th

Useless stuff

Haiku in English:
Entrepreneur's plea,
For support in wasteful times,
Echoes through the years.

Latin Translation:
Entreprenedoris preces,
Pro subsidio in temporibus prodigis,
Per annos resonant.

Reflection Prompt:

How can businesses balance profitability with sustainability?

Supplementary Content:

"Pro subsidio in temporibus prodigis" (for support in wasteful times)
highlights the ongoing appeal for support despite the environmental
cost, emphasizing the need for sustainable entrepreneurship.

November 10th

Useless stuff

Haiku in English:
Carbon footprint grows,
With each useless item sold,
Future's price is steep.

Latin Translation:
Vestigium carbonis crescit,
Cum unaquaque re inutili vendita,
Futuri pretium est grave.

Reflection Prompt:

What are some ways we can reduce our carbon footprint in our daily lives?

Supplementary Content:

"Futuri pretium est grave" (future's price is steep) underscores the significant long-term costs of current consumer behaviors, calling for immediate action to mitigate impact.

November 11th

Useless stuff

Haiku in English:
Corona reveals,
Trinkets are not life's essence,
Simplicity thrives.

Latin Translation:
Corona revelat,
Trinkets essentia vitae non sunt,
Simplicitate viget.

Reflection Prompt:

What aspects of simplicity did you find most rewarding during times of crisis?

Supplementary Content:

"Simplicitate viget" (simplicity thrives) emphasizes the value found in simplicity, a truth brought to light during the pandemic when many reassessed their priorities.

November 12th

Useless stuff

Haiku in English:
Useless items sell,
Despite environmental cost,
Change is overdue.

Latin Translation:
Res inutiles venduntur,
Praeter sumptus environmentalem,
Mutatio sero venit.

Reflection Prompt:

Why do you think there is a delay in implementing environmental changes despite awareness?

Supplementary Content:

"Mutatio sero venit" (change is overdue) reflects the urgency for environmental action, criticizing the lag in adopting sustainable practices despite known impacts.

November 13th

Useless stuff

Haiku in English:
Crisis clears the mind,
Essentials over excess,
Truth in simplicity.

Latin Translation:
Crisi mentem clarificat,
Essentialia supra excessum,
Veritas in simplicitate.

Reflection Prompt:

How can we maintain a focus on essentials as we move beyond times of crisis?

Supplementary Content:

"Veritas in simplicitate" (truth in simplicity) underscores the clarity gained during crises about what truly matters, advocating for a continued focus on essentials.

November 14th

Useless stuff

Haiku in English:
Wasteful habits die,
Hard in times of great excess,
Yet change starts with us.

Latin Translation:
Consuetudines prodigae moriuntur,
Difficiles in temporibus excessus,
Sed mutatio a nobis incipit.

Reflection Prompt:

What small changes can you make in your life to reduce waste?

Supplementary Content:

"Mutatio a nobis incipit" (change starts with us) highlights personal responsibility in driving environmental change, encouraging individual action to reduce waste.

November 15th

Useless stuff

Haiku in English:
Carbon warnings loud,
Still, the market thrums with waste,
Need for change is clear.

Latin Translation:
Monitiones carbonis clarae,
Tamen mercatus cum prodigo strepit,
Necessitas mutationis clara est.

Reflection Prompt:

How can market demand shift towards more sustainable products?

Supplementary Content:

"Necessitas mutationis clara est" (need for change is clear) emphasizes the evident need for environmental action, critiquing the market's ongoing wastefulness despite warnings.

November 16th

Useless stuff

Haiku in English:
Corona times teach,
Living light and free from waste,
Path to future's peace.

Latin Translation:
Tempora corona docent,
Vivere leve et sine prodigo,
Iter ad pacem futuram.

Reflection Prompt:

What lessons about sustainability did you learn during the pandemic?

Supplementary Content:

"Iter ad pacem futuram" (path to future's peace) highlights the sustainable practices learned during the pandemic, advocating for their continued application for a peaceful future.

November 17th

Useless stuff

Haiku in English:
Pushers of excess,
Blind to the environmental cost,
Earth bears the burden.

Latin Translation:
Venditores excessus,
Caeci ad sumptum environmentalem,
Terra onus fert.

Reflection Prompt:

What are the long-term impacts of ignoring environmental costs in business practices?

Supplementary Content:

"Terra onus fert" (Earth bears the burden) stresses the heavy toll on the planet from unchecked consumerism, calling for more environmentally conscious business practices.

November 18th

Useless stuff

Haiku in English:
Trinkets and trash sold,
Carbon footprints span the globe,
Lesson learned too late?

Latin Translation:
Trinkets et quisquiliae venduntur,
Vestigia carbonis globum amplectuntur,
Lectio sero didicerunt?

Reflection Prompt:

How can we ensure that lessons about sustainability are not learned too late?

Supplementary Content:

"Lectio sero didicerunt?" (lesson learned too late?) questions whether society will recognize the importance of sustainability before it's too late, urging timely action.

November 19th

Useless stuff

Haiku in English:
Support for wasteful,
Entrepreneurial ways,
Needs to find a halt.

Latin Translation:
Auxilium pro prodigis,
Viae entreprenoriales,
Fines inveniendum.

Reflection Prompt:

What strategies can be implemented to shift entrepreneurial efforts towards more sustainable practices?

Supplementary Content:

"Fines inveniendum" (needs to find a halt) highlights the necessity of ending support for wasteful business practices. This haiku and its translation encourage a reevaluation of how entrepreneurship can be aligned with sustainability goals.

November 20th

Useless stuff

Haiku in English:
Corona's clear sight,
Less is more in times of need,
Simplicity's grace.

Latin Translation:
Coronae clarus visus,
Minus est plus in necessitatibus,
Gratia simplicitatis.

Reflection Prompt:

What are some simple, sustainable habits you have adopted during times of need that you plan to continue?

Supplementary Content:

"Gratia simplicitatis" (simplicity's grace) emphasizes the beauty and effectiveness of simplicity, especially during challenging times. The haiku reflects on the lessons learned during the pandemic about the value of living with less.

November 21st

Envy

Haiku in English:
Jealousy brews hot,
Fate's unfair hand stirs the pot,
Cain's envy takes hold.

Latin Translation:
Invidia fervet,
Fortuna iniusta miscet,
Invidia Cain tenet.

Reflection Prompt:

Have you ever felt envy due to an unfair situation? How did you handle it?

Supplementary Content:

In this haiku, the intensity of Cain's envy is highlighted. The phrase "Fate's unfair hand" underscores the arbitrary nature of life's outcomes, which can ignite strong feelings of jealousy.

November 22nd

Envy

Haiku in English:
Gifts laid at God's feet,
One accepted, one denied,
Jealousy ignites.

Latin Translation:
Dona ante pedes Dei,
Unus acceptus, alter negatus,
Invidia incenditur.

Reflection Prompt:

Why do you think people respond differently to rejection? What emotions does it evoke in you?

Supplementary Content:

This haiku focuses on the pivotal moment of divine preference, which fuels Cain's jealousy. The ancient narrative underscores how perceived favoritism can lead to profound emotional reactions.

November 23rd

Envy

Haiku in English:
Abel's gift embraced,
Cain's offering left aside,
Dark envy emerges.

Latin Translation:
Abel munus acceptum,
Cain sacrificium relictum,
Nox invidia emergit.

Reflection Prompt:

Can you recall a time when you felt overshadowed by someone else's success? How did it affect you?

Supplementary Content:

The narrative of Cain and Abel is a classic example of sibling rivalry exacerbated by envy. The selective acceptance of offerings represents the deeper theme of arbitrary favor and its emotional impact.

November 24th

Envy

Haiku in English:
God's choice, a mystery,
Random fate's cruel decree,
Cain's heart fills with rage.

Latin Translation:
Electio Dei mysterium,
Cruel decretum fortunae,
Cor Cain iram implet.

Reflection Prompt:

Do you believe that life's outcomes are random or influenced by other factors? How do you cope with this uncertainty?

Supplementary Content:

The unpredictability of divine choice in this story illustrates the randomness of fate, a theme that resonates through many cultures and religions, often leading to feelings of injustice and anger.

November 25th

Envy

Haiku in English:
Sin knocks at the door,
Envy lurks in shadows deep,
Control it, God warns.

Latin Translation:
Peccatum ad ianuam pulsat,
Invidia in umbris latet,
Domina, Deus monet.

Reflection Prompt:

How do you manage feelings of envy when they arise? What strategies help you control them?

Supplementary Content:

God's warning to Cain about controlling his envy emphasizes the importance of self-awareness and restraint. This advice is timeless, reflecting universal wisdom on managing destructive emotions.

November 26th

Envy

Haiku in English:
Envy's bitter seed,
Planted deep within the heart,
Grows with silent pain.

Latin Translation:
Semina amara invidiae,
In corde alte plantata,
Crescit cum dolore tacito.

Reflection Prompt:

How does harboring envy affect your well-being and relationships?

Supplementary Content:

Envy, once rooted, can grow silently, causing significant internal suffering. This haiku captures the insidious nature of envy and its capacity to cause ongoing pain if not addressed.

November 27th

Envy

Haiku in English:
In Dante's dark swamp,
Envious souls lie buried,
Bubbles rise, unseen.

Latin Translation:
In palude obscura Dantis,
Animae invidae iacent,
Bullae surgunt, invisibiles.

Reflection Prompt:

What do you think Dante's portrayal of the envious signifies about the nature of envy?

Supplementary Content:

Dante's depiction of envious souls in his "Divine Comedy" symbolizes the concealed and corrosive nature of envy. The bubbles are a metaphor for suppressed feelings that still impact the soul.

November 28th

Envy

Haiku in English:
Grudges held so tight,
Bubbles of resentment rise,
In hell's murky depths.

Latin Translation:
Odium tenaciter,
Bullae odii surgunt,
In profundis inferni.

Reflection Prompt:

Have you ever held a grudge for a long time? What was the outcome?

Supplementary Content:

This haiku highlights the destructive potential of long-held grudges. Dante's imagery of bubbling resentment serves as a caution against allowing envy to fester unchecked.

November 29th

Envy

Haiku in English:
Envy's double edge,
Driving force for better deeds,
Yet, it cuts the soul.

Latin Translation:
Gladius duplex invidiae,
Vis ad meliora opera,
Sed, animam secat.

Reflection Prompt:

Can envy ever be positive? How can you channel it constructively?

Supplementary Content:

Envy can be a motivator for self-improvement but can also be deeply damaging. This dual nature is explored in many philosophical and literary works, reflecting its complex role in human behavior.

November 30th

Envy

Haiku in English:
Coveted new car,
Jealousy fuels desires,
Debt shadows the joy.

Latin Translation:
Novus currus desideratus,
Invidia desideria fovet,
Debitum umbram gaudii.

Reflection Prompt:

How do material desires influenced by envy impact your financial decisions?

Supplementary Content:

Modern consumerism often exploits envy to drive sales, leading to financial strain. This haiku reflects the cycle of desire and debt, a common consequence of material envy.

December 1st

Envy

Haiku in English:
Clothes to spark envy,
Marketed with sly intent,
Trapped in endless want.

Latin Translation:
Vestes invidiam excitantes,
Mercatus callide venditus,
In desiderio infinito capti.

Reflection Prompt:

In what ways does marketing use envy to influence your purchases?

Supplementary Content:

Advertising often targets our desire to be envied by others, trapping consumers in a cycle of never-ending wants. Understanding this can help us make more mindful purchasing decisions.

December 2nd

Envy

Haiku in English:
Progress, envy's child,
Striving for the higher mark,
Yet, never content.

Latin Translation:
Progressus, infans invidiae,
Ad summum contendens,
Numquam contentus.

Reflection Prompt:

How do you balance ambition with contentment?

Supplementary Content:

While envy can drive progress, it also perpetuates dissatisfaction. This haiku encourages reflection on finding a balance between striving for improvement and appreciating what one has.

December 3rd

Envy

Haiku in English:
Jealousy's green eye,
Sees only what others have,
Blinds to inner worth.

Latin Translation:
Oculus viridis invidiae,
Videns tantum quod alii habent,
Cecus ad internum valorem.

Reflection Prompt:

How can you shift focus from others' possessions to your own strengths?

Supplementary Content:

Jealousy often blinds us to our own value, focusing instead on others' possessions or achievements. Cultivating self-awareness and gratitude can help mitigate these feelings.

December 4th

Envy

Haiku in English:
Envy whispers low,
Tempts with false promises sweet,
Leads to hollow dreams.

Latin Translation:
Invidia submurmurat,
Falsa promissa dulcia temptat,
Ad somnia vacua ducit.

Reflection Prompt:

What false promises has envy tempted you with? How did you respond?

Supplementary Content:

Envy often entices with the illusion of fulfillment, leading to empty pursuits. Recognizing these false promises can help us seek more meaningful goals.

December 5th

Envy

Haiku in English:
Control envy's flame,
Channel it for noble aims,
Or be consumed whole.

Latin Translation:
Domina flammam invidiae,
Ad altos fines dirige,
Aut totus absorptus.

Reflection Prompt:

How can you transform feelings of envy into positive action?

Supplementary Content:

Learning to control and redirect envy can transform a potentially destructive emotion into a source of motivation for noble causes, fostering personal growth and achievement.

December 6th

Greed

Haiku in English:
Greed blinds the hungry,
Endless desire consumes,
Never satisfied.

Latin Translation:
Avaritia caecos,
Desiderium sine fine,
Numquam satis.

Reflection Prompt:

How do you recognize greed in your own life?

Supplementary Content:

Greed is often invisible to the person experiencing it. It can manifest as a constant need for more—whether it's money, possessions, or status. Reflecting on your desires can help you identify where greed may be influencing your actions.

December 7th

Greed

Haiku in English:
Fear whispers control,
Silencing the boldest hearts,
Intimidation.

Latin Translation:
Timor sussurrat,
Audacia corda tacet,
Metus imperat.

Reflection Prompt:

When has fear prevented you from speaking out?

Supplementary Content:

Fear can be a powerful tool for control. It often prevents people from taking action or speaking their truth. Understanding this can help you find courage in challenging situations.

December 8th

Greed

Haiku in English:
Revenge's dark embrace,
Binds the heart with bitter chains,
No peace in its grasp.

Latin Translation:
Ultio atra amplectitur,
Cor vinculis amarum,
Nulla pax in tenebris.

Reflection Prompt:

What are the consequences of seeking revenge?

Supplementary Content:

The desire for revenge can be consuming, leading to a cycle of bitterness and anger. Exploring the consequences of revenge can help you see the value of forgiveness and letting go.

December 9th

Greed

Haiku in English:
Nature's wealth abused,
Greed strips the earth's bounty bare,
Balance long forgotten.

Latin Translation:
Natura opes abusus,
Avaritia terram nudat,
Aequilibrium oblitus.

Reflection Prompt:

How does greed impact our environment?

Supplementary Content:

Greed drives overconsumption and exploitation of natural resources. Recognizing the impact of our actions on the environment can inspire more sustainable and balanced living.

December 10th

Greed

Haiku in English:
Minorities crushed,
By the weight of endless greed,
Justice cries in vain.

Latin Translation:
Minoritas oppressae,
Pondere avaritiae,
Justitia frustra clamat.

Reflection Prompt:

What can we do to support those marginalized by greed?

Supplementary Content:

Greed often leads to inequality, leaving marginalized communities to suffer. Reflecting on ways to support these communities can foster a more just and equitable society.

December 11th

Greed

Haiku in English:
Fear's shadow lingers,
Controlling the timid soul,
Courage breaks the chains.

Latin Translation:
Umbra timoris manet,
Animam timidam regit,
Virtus vincula frangit.

Reflection Prompt:

How can we overcome fear's control?

Supplementary Content:

Fear can linger and control our actions long after the initial threat is gone. Building courage through small acts of bravery can help break these chains and lead to greater freedom.

December 12th

Greed

Haiku in English:
Enough is a dream,
For the greedy heart's desire,
More is all it seeks.

Latin Translation:
Satis somnium est,
Cor avaritiae desiderat,
Magis solum quaerit.

Reflection Prompt:

What does "enough" mean to you?

Supplementary Content:

The concept of "enough" is subjective and can vary greatly between individuals. Reflecting on your own definition can help you find contentment and reduce the influence of greed.

December 13th

Greed

Haiku in English:
Revenge blinds the mind,
No clarity in its fire,
Wisdom lost to rage.

Latin Translation:
Ultio mentem caecat,
Nulla claritas in flamma,
Sapientia irae perdita.

Reflection Prompt:

Can you think of a time when you chose forgiveness over revenge?

Supplementary Content:

Choosing forgiveness over revenge can be incredibly challenging, but it often leads to personal growth and peace. Reflecting on past experiences can reinforce the value of forgiveness.

December 14th

Fear

Haiku in English:
Fear's effective rule,
Controls without a sound made,
Quiet submission.

Latin Translation:
Timor efficax regit,
Sine sono moderatur,
Tacita submissio.

Reflection Prompt:

How does fear manifest in society?

Supplementary Content:

Fear can manifest in many ways, from social norms to political power. Understanding these manifestations can help you see where fear is used as a tool for control in society.

December 15th

Greed

Haiku in English:
Greed's unending want,
Leaves the world in deep despair,
Sharing is the cure.

Latin Translation:
Avaritia sine fine,
Mundum in desolatione relinquit,
Communio remedium est.

Reflection Prompt:

How can sharing transform our communities?

Supplementary Content:

Sharing resources and wealth can create more balanced and supportive communities. Reflecting on the benefits of sharing can inspire actions that counteract greed.

December 16th

Greed

Haiku in English:
Nature's cry ignored,
For the greedy need much more,
Resources depleted.

Latin Translation:
Natura clamat neglecta,
Avaritia multum desiderat,
Opes exhauritae.

Reflection Prompt:

What can be done to protect our natural resources?

Supplementary Content:

Protecting natural resources requires awareness and action. Reflecting on individual and collective steps can help foster a more sustainable future.

December 17th

Greed

Haiku in English:
Sacred gold fames,
Money's lust blinds human hearts,
Never enough gold.

Latin Translation:
Auri sacra fames,
Pecuniae cupido caecos,
Numquam satis auri.

Reflection Prompt:

Why is the desire for money so powerful?

Supplementary Content:

The desire for money can overshadow other values and lead to destructive behaviors. Reflecting on why this desire is so powerful can help you understand its impact on your life.

December 18th

Greed

Haiku in English:
Revenge feeds on pain,
Grows with every bitter thought,
Consumes all within.

Latin Translation:
Ultio dolore alitur,
Crescens cum omni cogitatione amara,
Omnia absorbet.

Reflection Prompt:

How can we let go of grudges?

Supplementary Content:

Letting go of grudges can lead to greater peace and well-being. Reflecting on strategies for forgiveness can help you move past pain and anger.

December 19th

Greed

Haiku in English:
Greed's hunger for more,
Leaves the many with much less,
Fairness fades away.

Latin Translation:
Fames avaritiae magis,
Multis minus relinquit,
Aequitas evanescit.

Reflection Prompt:

How can fairness be restored in society?

Supplementary Content:

Restoring fairness requires addressing the root causes of inequality and greed. Reflecting on practical steps can guide efforts to create a more just society.

December 20th

Greed

Haiku in English:
Fear builds silent walls,
Around hearts that once were free,
Break them, let light in.

Latin Translation:
Timor muros tacitos construit,
Circa corda olim libera,
Frange eos, lucem admitte.

Reflection Prompt:
What steps can you take to overcome fear and live freely?

Supplementary Content:
Overcoming fear often involves confronting it directly and seeking support. Reflecting on practical steps can help you dismantle the barriers fear creates and embrace a freer life.

December 21st

Indoctrination

Haiku in English:
Truth sold in pieces,
Fragmented by hidden aims,
What is left of it?

Latin Translation:
Veritas vendita,
Partibus occultis scissa,
Quid restat ex ea?

Reflection Prompt:

How do you discern genuine information from marketing?

Supplementary Content:

In an age of information overload, it's crucial to question the sources
and motives behind the data we receive.

December 22nd

Indoctrination

Haiku in English:
Facts wrapped in sales pitch,
Hidden motives shape our views,
Clarity for sale.

Latin Translation:
Facta venditione,
Occultae causae visum formant,
Claritas venalis.

Reflection Prompt:

When has marketing influenced your perception of truth?

Supplementary Content:

Understanding how marketing techniques influence our beliefs can help us seek out more authentic information.

December 23rd

Indoctrination

Haiku in English:
Ideas for sale,
Thoughts branded with price tags,
Originals lost.

Latin Translation:
Idea venalis,
Cogitationes pretium habent,
Originalia perdita.

Reflection Prompt:

How do you protect your original thoughts in a marketed world?

Supplementary Content:

Reflecting on the commodification of ideas can inspire us to value and preserve originality in our thinking.

December 24th

Indoctrination

Haiku in English:
Security sold,
Fear packaged to generate,
Peace with a price tag.

Latin Translation:
Securitas vendita,
Timor pacatus generat,
Pax pretio signata.

Reflection Prompt:

What are the costs of buying a sense of security?

Supplementary Content:

Examining how security is marketed can reveal the underlying manipulation of fear in consumer culture.

December 25th

Indoctrination

Haiku in English:
Knowledge commodified,
Learning turned into profit,
True wisdom obscured.

Latin Translation:
Scientia commodificata,
Disciplina ad lucrum versa,
Sapientia vera obscurata.

Reflection Prompt:

How do you pursue genuine learning amidst commodified knowledge?

Supplementary Content:

Reflecting on the commercialization of education can guide us towards seeking more authentic and meaningful learning experiences.

December 26th

Indoctrination

Haiku in English:
Comfort sold in ads,
Luxury's promise beckons,
Simplicity lost.

Latin Translation:
Commoditas in nuntiis vendita,
Luxuriae promissio invitat,
Simplicitate perdita.

Reflection Prompt:

How does advertising shape your desires for comfort and luxury?

Supplementary Content:

Recognizing the influence of advertising can help us appreciate the
value of simplicity and contentment.

December 27th

Indoctrination

Haiku in English:
Opinions for sale,
Shaped by the highest bidder,
Where is our free thought?

Latin Translation:
Opiniones venales,
A summo emptore formatae,
Ubi nostra libera cogitatio?

Reflection Prompt:

How do you maintain independent thinking in a marketed world?

Supplementary Content:

Reflecting on the commodification of opinions can empower us to hold on to our independent judgments.

December 28th

Indoctrination

Haiku in English:
Happiness for sale,
Promised in each glossy page,
Contentment eludes.

Latin Translation:
Felicitas venalis,
In omni pagina lucida promissa,
Contentio fugit.

Reflection Prompt:

When has marketed happiness fallen short of true contentment?

Supplementary Content:

Exploring the disparity between marketed happiness and genuine contentment can help us prioritize what truly matters.

December 29th

Indoctrination

Haiku in English:
Services offered,
Peace of mind at a high cost,
Value redefined.

Latin Translation:
Officia oblata,
Pax animi pretio magno,
Valor redifinitus.

Reflection Prompt:

How do you evaluate the true worth of services offered to you?

Supplementary Content:

Reflecting on the true value of services can help us make more informed and meaningful choices.

December 30th

Indoctrination

Haiku in English:
Dreams packaged and sold,
Future's promise monetized,
Hope with a price tag.

Latin Translation:
Somnia vendita,
Promissio futuri monetata,
Spes pretio signata.

Reflection Prompt:

How does commercialization affect your personal dreams and aspirations?

Supplementary Content:

Considering how dreams are marketed can inspire us to protect and nurture our genuine aspirations.

December 31th

Indoctrination

Haiku in English:
Values advertised,
Moral goods with price tags fixed,
Integrity sold.

Latin Translation:
Valores nuntiati,
Bona moralia cum pretiis fixis,
Integritas vendita.

Reflection Prompt:

How do you maintain your values amidst commercial pressures?

Supplementary Content:

Reflecting on the marketing of values can strengthen our resolve to uphold our integrity.